Writing Strategies
for the Common Core

Integrating
Reading Comprehension
into the Writing Process

Grades 3–5

Hillary Wolfe, MA

Maupin House by
capstone®
professional

Writing Strategies for the Common Core:
Integrating Reading Comprehension into the Writing Process, Grades 3–5
By Hillary Wolfe, MA

© Copyright 2016. Hillary Wolfe, MA. All rights reserved.

Cover Design: Cynthia Della-Rovere
Book Design: Lisa King

Image Credits: Shutterstock: cover and interior

Library of Congress Cataloging-in-Publication Data
Cataloging-in-publication information is on file with the Library of Congress.

978-1-62521-934-3 (pbk.)
978-1-62521-944-2 (eBook PDF)
978-1-4966-0534-4 (eBook)

Maupin House publishes professional resources for K–12 educators. Contact us
for tailored, in-school training or to schedule an author for a workshop or conference.
Visit www.maupinhouse.com for free lesson plan downloads.

Maupin House Publishing, Inc. by Capstone Professional
1710 Roe Crest Drive
North Mankato, MN 56003

www.maupinhouse.com

888-262-6135

info@maupinhouse.com

Acknowledgments

I would very much like to thank my friends and editors at Capstone Professional, especially Karen Soll, Mary McCarthy, and David Willette. A special thank you also goes to Lynnette Brent Maddox. Everyone's faith and commitment to this project has been overwhelming.

I am grateful to my family, especially my husband Walt, and my children, Addie and Fletcher, for their patience and support.

I am especially thankful for all the teachers and students who have benefited from a structured approach to writing. Your tireless work inspires me daily.

Table of Contents

Introduction

During the decade before the creation of the Common Core State Standards, attention focused on effective strategies for teaching reading. Not as much was given to how to teach writing. Consequently, the curricula for students have been scattershot. A report to Carnegie Corporation of New York entitled "Writing Next: Effective Strategies to Improve Writing of Adolescents in Middle and High Schools" found that improving writing instruction for adolescents was "a topic that has previously not received enough attention from researchers or educators" (Graham & Perin, 2007, p. 3). However, the expectations put forth by the Common Core State Standards, in addition to the insurgence of new technology, intensified the need for instructional direction. "Writing, for adolescents who live in an age of digital communication, has taken on new importance and plays a prominent role in the way they socialize, share information, and structure their communication" (Sweeny, 2010, p. 121).

The finding was that there was still a lot of investigation that needed to be done to determine the best way to teach writing. The rich nature of the practice of writing and its relative neglect in instructional research make it inevitable that a whole compendium of possible approaches has not yet been studied. Research is clearly needed not only to identify additional effective practices that already exist but to develop new ones (Graham & Perin, 2007, p. 26).

What was evident was that "to be successful learners, adolescent readers must master complex texts, understand the diverse literacy demands of the different content areas, and navigate digital reading" (Biancarosa, 2012, p. 22). Therefore writing instruction, especially for adolescents, needed to be multipurpose. "Writing instruction for adolescents may involve process writing, along with instruction in different writing forms or genres, writing conventions and grammar, evaluation and criticism, and on-demand writing with prompts or for test purposes" (Sweeny, 2010, p. 125). For adolescents to master these complex tasks, writing instruction for grades three to five must build foundational knowledge and offer multiple opportunities to practice by writing for a variety of purposes, across all content areas.

Furthermore, writing has evolved to include a variety of modes of communication. "Writing is an integral part of students' lives today due to their use of texting and social networking sites, but most students do not recognize this type of communication as writing" (Sweeny, 2010, p. 124).

Balanced Literacy and Connecting Reading and Writing

The Common Core State Standards stressed "the importance of the reading-writing connection by requiring students to draw upon and write about evidence from literary and informational text" (Common Core State Standards Initiative, 2011, Standards for English Language Arts, p. 8).

Allington & Gabriel (2012) also described writing as connected to reading: "Writing provides a different modality within which to practice the skills and strategies of reading for an authentic purpose" (p. 13).

The most relevant research that has shown promise for both reading and writing instruction came from the balanced literacy model. Bitter, O'Day, et al. (2009) defined balanced literacy as an approach "designed to foster the gradual release of responsibility from teachers to students, moving from structured modeling (e.g., through read-alouds and shared reading) to scaffolded support (e.g., through guided reading) to independence of individual work" (p. 27). Balanced literacy models typically combined reading and writing instruction by integrating both instruction and practice in authentic settings and for relevant purposes. This integration enriched comprehension. "Students need to learn strategies to support their comprehension, not to demonstrate the acquisition of a new skill" (Guccione, 2011, p. 575). Furthermore, research has shown that an integrated approach was preferable to a single "silver bullet" solution to literacy instruction for adolescent readers: "There is no magic bullet or one-size-fits-all approach to improving adolescent literacy learning....Current policy texts may not propose a single solution, but they do advocate a number of interventions or programs as needed reforms" (Franzak, 2006, p. 236).

There are many different approaches to literacy available to teachers. "Although there are many best practices for teaching students to read...the challenge is in knowing which instructional strategy to choose" (Miller & Veatch, 2010, p. 154).

Why I Wrote This Book and How to Use It

An examination of different implementation models of balanced literacy led to the creation of this curriculum, consisting of four chapters. Three chapters address a text type (or genre) as defined by the Common Core State Standards for Writing—"Explanatory/Informational," "Argument," and "Narrative"—with another chapter, "Response to Literature," included because many standardized tests require students to quickly respond to a poem or short narrative. "Response to Literature" is an umbrella category, in that it can encompass any of the text types. But the Common Core State Standards demand that students become accustomed to citing evidence from a piece of text and engaging in the close reading and analysis of text as part of the writing process. Chapters on the reading/writing connection and test prep round out this resource.

Within each of the three genre units, blocks of core instruction are combined to be delivered over a four- to six-week time period and sample lessons are provided as models for instruction. Two Mini-lessons are included for each of three strategies per genre. The chapters on the reading/writing connection, response to literature, and test prep also contain additional strategies and Mini-lessons. Mini-lessons provide applicable Common Core Standards, materials lists, overviews, planning tips, procedures (including modeling, guided practice, and independent practice opportunities), reading connections, formative assessments, and reproducible graphic organizers and rubrics (both analytic for formative assessments and holistic for summative assessments).

The classroom setting for a balanced literacy model of instruction reflects constructivist principles, in which the students take more ownership of learning the strategies and skills they will need to apply across multiple content areas. "Constructivism recognizes that learning occurs most often in a social setting; thus, the formation of a classroom…is vital to student success" Saulnier, 2008, p. 6). A classroom built to accommodate balanced literacy looks different from a traditional classroom with desks in rows. It also operates differently, as students must transition more frequently between whole-group, small-group, paired, and independent work areas. Therefore, setting up the classroom and instructional plan requires a new approach. "Our teaching behaviors, our expectations we set for our students, and our students' learning behaviors must evolve to fit our students' futures" (Saulnier, 2008, p. 7).

Integrating all the components of a balanced literacy framework also requires some backward planning. The teacher must choose an overall objective and then smaller benchmark objectives that serve as prerequisites to reach the overarching goal. There also must be time for assessment (both formative and summative) and reteaching when necessary. According to Wiggins & McTighe, learning for understanding develops in an iterative fashion across the three categories of transfer, meaning, and acquisition. "The acquisition of new vocabulary [is] introduced in response to real problems … and as preparation for the final performance task. … The unit culminates in a thought-provoking (and personally relevant) transfer task and a reflection on the unit's essential questions" (2008, p. 38).

Structuring the Class for Balanced Literacy

According to Bitter, O'Day, et al. (2009), a balanced literacy model fosters comprehension by integrating reading and writing in both instruction and practice, in authentic settings and for relevant purposes. This approach allows for the gradual release of responsibility from teacher to student. They describe a classroom setting that offers structured modeling, scaffolded support through small-group guided practice, and opportunities for independent practice. Not only is this arrangement better suited for an integrated curriculum, it also helps promote students' self-efficacy. Swafford & Durrington (2010) explained that "the instructional practices utilized by teachers have an impact on both [self-efficacy and achievement]" (p. 222). They cite research that shows that when instructional practices included teacher modeling, guided practice, and independent practice, learners were more likely to perform a new task successfully, and more importantly, were more likely to tackle and accomplish a difficult task. These practices raised self-efficacy (as cited in Bandura, 1997; Schunk, 2003; Schunk & Pajares, 2005; Schunk & Zimmerman, 2007).

Logistically, this structure works best in a classroom where students have regular opportunities to engage in center or workstation activities, as well as time to work independently, with partners, or as a whole class. Goal-setting and conferencing requires the teacher to have time to work one on one with students, uninterrupted and free from distraction. In order to create a chaos-free environment, the teacher must strategize.

The following tips can help establish and streamline classroom management procedures.

Room Arrangement

Prepare your students for different group structures by teaching and practicing procedures for group arrangements.

Whole Class

Consider if you want your students sitting in rows. Rows hinder the teacher from maintaining proximity with students, which is a key strategy for minimizing disruption. If your room allows it, consider having desks facing each other. This arrangement takes away the "back of the room" and gives the teacher quick and equal access to all students.

Consider placing desks in pods. Writing is just one of the language skills students are learning. They also need to practice speaking and listening, and collaborating and communicating effectively (Common Core). "Students suggested that collaboration with partner, small group, or the teacher would be helpful to develop oral reading confidence" (Swafford & Durrington, 2010, p. 231). Capitalize on this fact by setting up heterogeneous table groups. Each group can work as a team, and the teacher can create a reward system that encourages cooperation. Individual effort is still expected and can contribute to the success of the team. This strategy gives students ownership and responsibility for their work, and can be more engaging and intrinsically motivating. Swafford & Durrington state, "To become self-efficacious readers,...students needed to experience reading in an instructional context in which they felt supported" (2010, p. 230).

Small Group

Encourage flexible grouping by instructing students how to quickly and efficiently move their desks to work in pairs, in triads, or in groups of four or five. Use symbols to represent various configurations; for example, two circles represent partner work, a triangle means they are to work in groups of three, a square means work in groups of four, and a five-pointed star means work in a group of five. Have students practice picking up and moving their desks to get into the appropriate formations. Be prepared to practice these configurations multiple times at first, and to revisit the practice periodically through the year. Students should be expected to move their desks simply, quickly, and quietly. Once they have the procedure down pat, simply write the appropriate symbol on the board and students will know without questioning how they are to arrange themselves for the day.

Move the station, not the students. Keep practice assignments for small-group work in laminated pocket folders or sturdy boxes or bags. Give students 10 to 15 minutes to work on one task, then move the folders or boxes to the next table. Continue working this way until all students have had a chance to complete each station's assignment. One station should be set aside for time with the teacher to address intervention or guided practice.

Independent Practice

If possible, provide some comfortable areas for students to work on their own. Beanbags, a futon in the corner, or even individual computer stations with inviting lighting will set the stage for a relaxing environment. If you must have desks in rows, keep the struggling learners in front, closest to you. This will help you stay focused on those students who need more guidance and direct instruction. Be sure to rearrange students at the start of each unit so everyone has a chance to benefit from more attention from the teacher.

Using Reading and Writing Portfolios

According to Swafford & Durrington (2010), adolescents need to take ownership of their work. "There is an increasing demand on students as 21st century learners to take responsibility to continue learning outside of school, so it is extremely important for teachers to help them become self-efficacious readers" (p. 232). Using a reading and writing portfolio gives younger students strategies for keeping track of notes and staying accountable for assignments. Here are some tips for creating and using reading and writing portfolios in class.

Be Practical

A portfolio can be as simple as six sheets of notebook paper folded in half and stapled together. Use sturdy paper to add pockets. A portfolio only needs to last for four weeks or as long as one unit of instruction.

Have students turn in their portfolios as a form of assessment. This work product will provide more information than a report card to parents about how the student progressed through the unit.

Make a Cover Page

Let students decorate and label their portfolios as they want (within reason, of course). Leave the first page blank so students can create a table of contents either as they go or at the end of the unit. Creating a table of contents can be a form of summarizing what students have learned and can serve as a study tool.

Keep the Portfolios in Class

Since these tools will be used daily, students need guaranteed access to them. Find a magazine holder or a basket and color code each one to correspond with each table or group. At the beginning of class, students retrieve their portfolios, and at the end, they replace them in the basket. Organize the portfolios so that all reading information is on the right side (R=right=reading) and all the writing information is on the left side. That will help students when they are trying to find information quickly.

Working Backward

Wiggins & McTighe (2011) described a method of instructional planning that worked backward: "1) focus on teaching and assessing for understanding and learning transfer, and 2) design curriculum 'backward' from those ends" (p. 1). That is, teachers think of what they want their students to have achieved at the end of the unit, and then fill in the necessary assignments and checkpoints needed to reach that goal.

Each unit of instruction in this strategies notebook follows a balanced literacy framework and includes the following:

- Modeled reading instruction
- Guided reading practice
- Independent reading
- Modeled writing instruction
- Guided writing practice
- Independent writing
- Vocabulary (direct instruction of word analysis and decoding strategies)
- Content-area vocabulary (embedded in reading and writing practice)

Creating a Planning Calendar

Use the following steps to create a four-week planning calendar for teaching the strategies in this book.

Start with a Culminating Assignment

The culminating assignment for each unit reflects that specific form of writing. For example, a culminating assignment for the explanatory/informational unit could be a class newspaper, a student-authored textbook, or an essay. A culminating assignment for the argument unit could be a commercial, an editorial, or a community campaign. For the narrative unit, students could write a story, create a short video, or put on a play as a culminating experience.

The culminating assignment can also integrate content-area themes. For example, by combining mathematics and argument, students could conduct surveys, chart their data in a specific type of graph, then write a convincing argument using the data they collected. In science, students could write a narrative from the perspective of a comet in the universe and describe its journey as it travels through the solar system. In social studies, students could be writing collaboratively or with a partner, explaining a historical event from a number of different perspectives.

Once the culminating assignment has been decided, write it in your planning calendar at the end of the third week. The fourth week of the unit should be saved for revisions, test preparation, and reteaching. The summative assessment should take place in the middle of the week, so there is still time to make up work, allow students to make presentations, or revisit a skill and get ready for the next unit.

Planning Calendar 1

	Monday	Tuesday	Wednesday	Thursday	Friday
Week 1					
Week 2					
Week 3					
Week 4	Culminating assignment due	Presentations and reteaching	Summative assessment	Make-up presentations	Make-up presentations

Fill in Reading Instruction/Reading Practice

The purpose for a culminating assignment is to allow students to synthesize and integrate all the specific characteristics of that genre. Consider all the skills students will need to successfully master the text type. Narrow the focus to only include the most important five or six. (Use your pacing guide or the criteria in the Common Core State Standards as your guide, and collaborate with your grade level team during common planning time.) Start the unit with an overview of the genre, and then fill in the reading instruction so that one strategy is covered every three to five days.

For example, informational text "organizes the explanation in successive steps, using imperative verbs...." (Duke, Caughlan, et al., 2012, pp. 37–38). Therefore in the Explanatory unit, students will practice the following:

- Visualize while reading
- Monitor understanding by predicting
- Determine a main idea
- Distinguish a significant from an insignificant detail
- Summarize information

Each of these strategies would be addressed individually as shown on the planning calendar below. Allow one or two days after the instruction for guided practice.

Fill in Writing Instruction/Writing Practice

Integrate writing into the equation and reinforce the reading and writing connection by weaving writing strategies into the calendar. This will give students opportunities to write for different purposes and time frames, as specified by the Common Core State Standards for grades three through five: "Write routinely over extended time frames (time for research, reflection, and revision) and shorter time frames (a single sitting or a day or two) for a range of discipline-specific tasks, purposes, and audiences" (Corestandards.org, p. 44).

For example, in the explanatory unit, if students are practicing the reading strategy of visualizing while reading, follow that lesson with a writing exercise focused on using descriptive sensory words. Give students a day after modeling to work in small groups or individually to write a descriptive piece. (See the planning calendar below.)

Planning Calendar 2

	Monday	Tuesday	Wednesday	Thursday	Friday
Week 1	RI: Visualize	RP: Guided practice	WI: Descriptive writing	WP: Descriptive writing	RI: Predict
Week 2	RP: Guided practice	WI: Cause and effect	WP: Cause and effect	RI: Main idea and detail RP: Guided practice	WI: Main idea and detail
Week 3	WP: Main idea and detail	RI: Summary	RP: Guided practice	WI: Summary culminating assignment draft	WP: Summary culminating assignment draft
Week 4	CA: Due	Presentations and reteaching	Summative assessment	Make-up presentations	Make-up presentations

Legend

RI = Reading Instruction
WI = Writing Instruction
RP = Reading Practice
WP = Writing Practice
CA = Culminating Assignment

Fill in Vocabulary and Grammar

Vocabulary can be addressed in two ways. First, provide explicit and direct word analysis and decoding strategies as an opening activity two to five days each week, for 10–15 minutes at a time. Fill in this time on your planning calendar. Include vocabulary checks on each Friday.

Next, provide content-specific vocabulary instruction within the structure of reading and writing. This can be done as an explicit reading strategy (to look for transition words or active verbs, for example), or as a writing strategy (as part of revising and editing within the writing process). Limit vocabulary to five to eight words at a time, and provide opportunities for practice through word consciousness and word awareness activities.

Time for Reteaching

The final week of the unit can be saved for reteaching, but also allow flexibility within the other weeks of the unit for a quick 20- to 30-minute review as needed. Use formative assessments regularly, and use the information gained from these tools to determine whether students are ready to move on or if they need more scaffolded instruction. Ideas for formative assessments are included with each strategy.

Test Prep

Synthesize the unit for students and show them the relevance of the information by practicing test prep. Help students identify the key words in a prompt that will alert them to what their response should contain. Have them practice with a few prompts at the end of the unit.

Next, show students how to use all the tools they learned throughout the unit to quickly organize a written response or to skim a reading passage for pertinent information.

Planning Calendar 3

	Monday	Tuesday	Wednesday	Thursday	Friday
Week 1	ML: Vocabulary RI: Visualize	RP: Guided practice	ML: Vocabulary WI: Descriptive writing	WP: Descriptive writing	RI: Predict
Week 2	ML: Vocabulary RP: Guided practice	WI: Cause and effect	ML: Vocabulary WP: Cause and effect	RI: Main idea and detail RP: Guided practice	WI: Main idea and detail
Week 3	ML: Grammar WP: Main idea and detail	RI: Summary	RP: Guided practice	ML: Grammar WI: Summary culminating assignment draft	WP: Summary culminating assignment draft
Week 4	CA: Due	Presentations and reteaching	Summative assessment	Test prep and make-up presentations	Test prep and make-up presentations

Legend

ML = Mini-lesson   WI = Writing Instruction

RI = Reading Instruction   WP = Writing Practice

RP = Reading Practice   CA = Culminating Assignment

Standards Correlations

The lessons in this book are correlated to the Common Core State Standards for Reading and Writing. Grade 5 writing standards are included to represent the standards for the grades 3–5 band.

Common Core Anchor Standards

Anchor Standards	Lesson(s)
CCSS.ELA-Literacy.CCRA.R.1 Read closely to determine what the text says explicitly and to make logical inferences from it; cite specific textual evidence when writing or speaking to support conclusions drawn from the text.	All lessons
CCSS.ELA-Literacy.CCRA.R.2 Determine central ideas or themes of a text and analyze their development; summarize the key supporting details and ideas.	All lessons
CCSS.ELA-Literacy.CCRA.R.3 Analyze how and why individuals, events, or ideas develop and interact over the course of a text.	All lessons
CCSS.ELA-Literacy.CCRA.R.4 Interpret words and phrases as they are used in a text, including determining technical, connotative, and figurative meanings, and analyze how specific word choices shape meaning or tone.	All lessons
CCSS.ELA-Literacy.CCRA.R.5 Analyze the structure of texts, including how specific sentences, paragraphs, and larger portions of the text (e.g., a section, chapter, scene, or stanza) relate to each other and the whole.	All lessons
CCSS.ELA-Literacy.CCRA.R.6 Assess how point of view or purpose shapes the content and style of a text.	All lessons
CCSS.ELA-Literacy.CCRA.R.7 Integrate and evaluate content presented in diverse media and formats, including visually and quantitatively, as well as in words.	All lessons
CCSS.ELA-Literacy.CCRA.R.8 Delineate and evaluate the argument and specific claims in a text, including the validity of the reasoning as well as the relevance and sufficiency of the evidence.	All lessons
CCSS.ELA-Literacy.CCRA.R.9 Analyze how two or more texts address similar themes or topics in order to build knowledge or to compare the approaches the authors take.	All lessons
CCSS.ELA-Literacy.CCRA.R.10 Read and comprehend complex literary and informational texts independently and proficiently.	All lessons
CCSS.ELA-Literacy.CCRA.W.1 Write arguments to support claims in an analysis of substantive topics or texts using valid reasoning and relevant and sufficient evidence.	Mini-lesson: Characteristics of Argument Text (p. 27)
CCSS.ELA-Literacy.CCRA.W.2 Write informative/explanatory texts to examine and convey complex ideas and information clearly and accurately through the effective selection, organization, and analysis of content.	Mini-lesson: Characteristics of Explanatory/ Informational Text (p. 21)
CCSS.ELA-Literacy.CCRA.W.3 Write narratives to develop real or imagined experiences or events using effective technique, well-chosen details and well-structured event sequences.	Mini-lesson: Characteristics of Narrative Text (p. 31)
CCSS.ELA-Literacy.CCRA.W.4 Produce clear and coherent writing in which the development, organization, and style are appropriate to task, purpose, and audience.	All lessons

Common Core Anchor Standards

Anchor Standards	Lesson(s)
CCSS.ELA-Literacy.CCRA.W.5 Develop and strengthen writing as needed by planning, revising, editing, rewriting, or trying a new approach.	All lessons
CCSS.ELA-Literacy.CCRA.W.6 Use technology, including the Internet, to produce and publish writing and to interact and collaborate with others.	All lessons
CCSS.ELA-Literacy.CCRA.W.7 Conduct short as well as more sustained research projects based on focused questions, demonstrating understanding of the subject under investigation.	All lessons
CCSS.ELA-Literacy.CCRA.W.8 Gather relevant information from multiple print and digital sources, assess the credibility and accuracy of each source, and integrate the information while avoiding plagiarism.	Mini-lesson: How Appealing! (p. 53)
CCSS.ELA-Literacy.CCRA.W.9 Draw evidence from literary or informational texts to support analysis, reflection, and research.	Mini-lesson: Text Features and Significant Details (p. 45)
CCSS.ELA-Literacy.CCRA.W.10 Write routinely over extended time frames (time for research, reflection, and revision) and shorter time frames (a single sitting or a day or two) for a range of tasks, purposes, and audiences.	All lessons

Common Core State Standards for Writing

Grade 5 Standards Represent Grades 3–5	Lesson(s)
CCSS.ELA-Literacy.W.1 Write opinion pieces on topics or texts, supporting a point of view with reasons and information. **CCSS.ELA-Literacy.W.1a** Introduce a topic or text clearly, state an opinion, and create an organizational structure in which ideas are logically grouped to support the writer's purpose. **CCSS.ELA-Literacy.W.1b** Provide logically ordered reasons that are supported by facts and details. **CCSS.ELA-Literacy.W.1c** Link opinion and reasons using words, phrases, and clauses (e.g., *consequently*, *specifically*). **CCSS.ELA-Literacy.W.1d** Provide a concluding statement or section related to the opinion presented.	Mini-lesson: Characteristics of Argument Text (p. 27); Prewriting Mini-lesson: Facts and Opinions (p. 117); Prewriting Mini-lesson: Supporting Details (p. 121); Drafting Mini-lesson: Thematic Writing (p. 126); Drafting Mini-lesson: Structuring an Argument (p. 129); Revising Mini-lesson: Transitions (p. 134); Revising Mini-lesson: Linking Ideas (p. 138); Test Prep Mini-lesson: Determine the Task (Argument) (p. 202); Test Prep Mini-lesson: Stake Your Claim (Argument) (p. 210)
CCSS.ELA-Literacy.W.2 Write informative/ explanatory texts to examine a topic and convey ideas and information clearly. **CCSS.ELA-Literacy.W.2a** Introduce a topic clearly, provide a general observation and focus, and group related information logically; include formatting (e.g., headings), illustrations, and multimedia when useful to aiding comprehension. **CCSS.ELA-Literacy.W.2b** Develop the topic with facts, definitions, concrete details, quotations, or other information and examples related to the topic. **CCSS.ELA-Literacy.W.2c** Link ideas within and across categories of information using words, phrases, and clauses (e.g., *in contrast, especially*). **CCSS.ELA-Literacy.W.2d** Use precise language and domain-specific vocabulary to inform about or explain the topic. **CCSS.ELA-Literacy.W.2e** Provide a concluding statement or section related to the information or explanation presented.	Mini-lesson: Characteristics of Explanatory/ Informational Text (p. 21); Mini-lesson: Main Ideas and Details (p. 37); Mini-lesson: Topic and Concluding Sentences (p. 40); Prewriting Mini-lesson: Observations (p. 74); Prewriting Mini-lesson: Processes (p. 78); Drafting Mini-lesson: Openings (p. 84); Drafting Mini-lesson: Closings (p. 87); Revising Mini-lesson: Words That Explain (p. 93); Revising Mini-lesson: Sentence Structure (p. 99); Test Prep Mini-lesson: Determine the Task (Explanatory/ Informational) (p. 198); Test Prep Mini-lesson: Create a Thesis (Explanatory/Informational) (p. 206)

Common Core State Standards for Writing

Grade 5 Standards Represent Grades 3–5	Lesson(s)
CCSS.ELA-Literacy.W.3 Write narratives to develop real or imagined experiences or events using effective technique, descriptive details, and clear event sequences. **CCSS.ELA-Literacy.W.3a** Orient the reader by establishing a situation and introducing a narrator and/or characters; organize an event sequence that unfolds naturally. **CCSS.ELA-Literacy.W.3b** Use narrative techniques, such as dialogue, description, and pacing, to develop experiences and events or show the responses of characters to situations. **CCSS.ELA-Literacy.W.3c** Use a variety of transitional words, phrases, and clauses to manage the sequence of events. **CCSS.ELA-Literacy.W.3d** Use concrete words and phrases and sensory details to convey experiences and events precisely. **CCSS.ELA-Literacy.W.3e** Provide a conclusion that follows from the narrated experiences or events.	Mini-lesson: Characteristics of Narrative Text (p. 31); Mini-lesson: Literary Devices (p. 64); Prewriting Mini-lesson: Story Structures (p. 156); Prewriting Mini-lesson: Character Traits (p. 161); Drafting Mini-lesson: Shared Writing (p. 166); Drafting Mini-lesson: Sensibility (p. 170); Revising Mini-lesson: Sentence Complexity with Clauses (p. 177); Revising Mini-lesson: Conclusions (p. 182); Test Prep Mini-lesson: Determine the Task (Narrative) (p. 204); Test Prep Mini-lesson: Plot and Character (Narrative) (p. 214)
CCSS.ELA-Literacy.W.4 Produce clear and coherent writing in which the development and organization are appropriate to task, purpose, and audience.	All lessons
CCSS.ELA-Literacy.W.5 With guidance and support from peers and adults, develop and strengthen writing as needed by planning, revising, editing, rewriting, or trying a new approach.	All lessons
CCSS.ELA-Literacy.W.6 With some guidance and support from adults, use technology, including the Internet, to produce and publish writing as well as to interact and collaborate with others; demonstrate sufficient command of keyboarding skills to type a minimum of two pages in a single sitting.	All lessons
CCSS.ELA-Literacy.W.7 Conduct short research projects that use several sources to build knowledge through investigation of different aspects of a topic.	All lessons
CCSS.ELA-Literacy.W.8 Recall relevant information from experiences or gather relevant information from print and digital sources; summarize or paraphrase information in notes and finished work, and provide a list of sources.	All lessons
CCSS.ELA-Literacy.W.9 Draw evidence from literary or informational texts to support analysis, reflection, and research. **CCSS.ELA-Literacy.W.9a** Apply *grade 5 reading standards* to literature (e.g., "Compare and contrast two or more characters, settings, or events in a story or a drama, drawing on specific details in the text [e.g., how characters interact]"). **CCSS.ELA-Literacy.W.9b** Apply *grade 5 reading standards* to informational texts (e.g., "Explain how an author uses reasons and evidence to support particular points in a text, identifying which reasons and evidence support which point[s]").	All lessons

Common Core State Standards for Writing

Grade 5 Standards Represent Grades 3–5	Lesson(s)
CCSS.ELA-Literacy.W.10 Write routinely over extended time frames (time for research, reflection, and revision) and shorter time frames (a single sitting or a day or two) for a range of discipline-specific tasks, purposes, and audiences.	All lessons

Chapter 1

The Reading/ Writing Connection

Overview: Understanding Text Types and Purposes

Why connect reading and writing instructionally? A recent report to Carnegie Corporation of New York, *Writing to Read*, identified "instructional practices shown to be effective in improving students' reading" (Graham & Hebert, 2010, p. 5). The report recommended that students write about what they read; learn and practice the steps of the writing process; and write for extended periods of time.

This strategy section aims to provide a road map for choosing reading materials that will support the specific skills and structures of each particular text type. By practicing writing within text types and understanding the characteristics of that type, students will recognize those characteristics when they read. More importantly, they will recognize the characteristics across content areas, increasing their comprehension in other subjects.

The first step in this process is to recognize the features and characteristics of each of the three text types outlined in the Common Core State Standards:

- Explanatory or informational text
- Argument (also called opinion writing at elementary)
- Narrative

Explanatory text is the first genre addressed because it is the most objective form of writing. The characteristics are easy to identify in multiple contexts and content areas, and the skills needed to write effective informational text are straightforward. By starting with explanatory text, students get a chance to feel successful with a writing task that feels very doable, and the emotional risk involved in writing is minimized.

Explanatory text is also the most prevalent kind of text students will encounter outside of school. Technical documents, applications, and résumés are just some of the examples of the kind of text that students will encounter, both as a reader and as a writer.

Finally, informational text is easily assessed because it lends itself to a more formulaic structure. Teachers can ease into using an analytic rubric by assessing very specific elements. Similarly, students can serve as peer reviewers when they have a very clear set of criteria by which to judge another student's writing.

Note: Unless noted otherwise, you will need to provide enough copies of the reproducibles mentioned in the materials lists for each student in class.

Mini-lesson: Characteristics of Explanatory/Informational Text

Materials

- Colored paper
- Chart paper
- Building blocks or small, plastic bricks
- Wind-up toys or paddle balls
- Plastic animals or dinosaurs
- *Can You Explain?* activity sheets (one for each pair or group of 4 students), pages 24–25
- *Text Types and Purposes Chart* (optional), page 26

Overview

Students will be introduced to characteristics and types of explanatory writing. They will create a graphic organizer to help them remember the characteristics and use the characteristics to help improve their own informational writing.

Planning

Set up stations ahead of time by having different kinds of toys and objects in bins or plastic bags. Depending on the size of your class, you may consider having students stay in their seats but move the bags around instead. In this case, be sure you have enough materials for each pair or group of students.

Take time to define the roles of each group member: Recorder writes all the information on the activity sheet, investigator performs all the experiments, questioner/narrator reads the instructions or asks questions that the investigator must solve, presenter will be responsible for sharing the group's findings at the end of the activity.

Procedure

Modeling

1. Tell students that they will be learning about explanatory writing. Have students work with partners or groups of four, and distribute one sheet of colored paper to each student. Have students fold the paper in half length-wise, then fold each edge toward the middle (thirds). Use scissors to cut each flap.

2. Write the words "explanatory" and "informational" on the board, and ask students to write those words at the top of their folded colored paper. Ask students if they recognize any word within those words (explain, inform). Tell students that explanatory or informational text explains something.

3. Use a document camera to display a passage of explanatory text (how-to instructions). Read the text aloud and ask students what this text is explaining (how to do something). Tell students to write "Explains HOW" on the first flap (left). Have students open the flap and brainstorm with their partner or group about some of the characteristics of how-to text. (Guide students to include clear descriptions, step-by-step instructions, either a process or directions, and sometimes visuals.)

4. Write a shared definition on a sheet of chart paper, and ask each student to copy this definition under the first flap on the paper. Have them leave some room in case they need to add information later.

5. Use a document camera to display a short passage of text that explains a cause-effect relationship. Read the text aloud and ask students what this text is explaining (explains why). Have students work together to brainstorm some of the characteristics of this text (shows the reasons, explains outcomes, uses facts and descriptions, visuals). Chart their responses and have students copy the characteristics under the second flap. Remind them to leave some room in case they need to add information later.

6. Use a document camera to display a short passage that compares two items. Read the text aloud and ask students what this text is explaining (explains similarities and differences). Have students work together to brainstorm some of the characteristics of this text (gives equal attention to two things, shows pros and cons of each). Chart their responses and have students copy the characteristics under the third flap. Again, have them leave some room in case they need to add information later.

Guided Practice

7. Set up three stations around the room. At station 1, have several sets of building or construction materials (e.g., blocks). At station 2, have a variety of wind-up toys, paddle balls, etc. At station 3, have several different plastic animals, such as dinosaurs or mammals.

8. Distribute blank copies of the *Can You Explain?* activity sheets, one per group. Have students fill in the names of each group member and define their roles.

    Send groups of students to each station. Tell students that each group will be asked to work together to complete the activity sheet. Then, after 10 minutes, they will rotate to a new station. Have groups choose someone to be the recorder.

    At station 1, students will build a structure and then write the step-by-step directions in the appropriate boxes on the activity sheet. At station 2, students will observe how the toys work and then fill in the cause-and-effect frame on their activity sheet. At station 3, students will choose two different animals and compare them using the sentence frames on their activity sheets.

9. Once all groups have completed all stations, choose a volunteer to share the instructions for how to build a sculpture (station 1). Ask another volunteer to try to recreate the structure by listening to the directions.

10. Ask the listener what was easy or what was difficult about the instructions (e.g., It's easier to follow when the steps are in order, when the pieces are described clearly; it's difficult when the directions are vague). Have students turn to a partner and tell what is important to remember about explaining a process. Chart their answers and have students add information under the "Explains HOW" flap.

11. Choose a different volunteer to explain why one of the toys at station 2 works the way it does, without identifying the toy. Ask the class to guess which toy was being described. Refer to the "Explains HOW" chart. Did the same characteristics help when describing a cause and effect? Ask students to share their ideas with a partner, then chart their responses on the "Explains WHY" chart and ask students to add information under that flap on their colored sheets.

12. Choose another volunteer to explain how two plastic animals were similar or different, without naming the animals. Ask the class to guess which two animals were described. What were the clues that helped the class guess the answer (e.g., clear descriptions, specific language, facts)?

13. Tell students they have just described the important characteristics of informational or explanatory text.

Independent Practice

14. Tell students that the first thing we do as readers is to determine the purpose of the text. The purpose of informational or explanatory text will be to explain how, to explain why, and to explain similarities and differences.

15. Have students discuss what they have discovered about informational text.

16. Chart their answers. (Guide students to write things such as, "sequential," "specific details," "clear descriptions.")

17. Distribute a copy of nonfiction explanatory text to partners. Ask them to read the text together and decide if the text is explaining how, why (cause-effect), or comparing similarities and differences. Quiz the class, and have them show with a thumbs-up or small, individual whiteboards or colored cards which purpose is being addressed by each piece of text.

18. Have students write an explanation in their own words of explanatory or informational text. Remind them to use the information they added under the flaps on the colored papers they created.

Optional: Have students paste the *Text Types and Purposes Chart* in their portfolios. Have students fill it out as they learn about each text type.

Characteristics of Explanatory or Informational Text

Recorder: _____

Investigator: _____

Presenter: _____

Questioner/Narrator: _____

Can You Explain?

Directions: Choose your role and write your name on the line above. At each station, work together to complete the assigned task. Use the sentence frames below to help you.

Station 1:

Work together to build a structure. Write the step-by-step process in the boxes below. Remember, another team will attempt to recreate your structure. Your process should include at least five steps.

First, _____.
Next, _____.
Then, _____.
After that, _____.
Finally, _____.

©2016 Hillary Wolfe, MA from *Writing Strategies for the Common Core*. This page may be reproduced for classroom use only.

Station 2:

Choose one mechanical toy or game. Work together to describe what causes the toy or game to work. Another team will attempt to guess which toy or game you are describing, so do not name it, but try to make your descriptions as clear as possible.

The purpose of this (toy/game) is _____.

It works by first _____.

When _____ happens,

then _____.

If _____,

then the result is _____.

Station 3:

Choose two animals and work with your group to describe ways they are similar and ways they are different. You may not use the names of the animals in your descriptions. Another team will try to guess which two animals you chose.

The first animal has _____.

and _____.

It also has _____.

It is similar to the second animal because they both _____

_____

and _____.

But it is different because _____

_____

and because _____.

Characteristics of Text Types

Name: _____

Text Types and Purposes Chart

	Informational/Explanation	Argument	Narrative
Purpose			
Features			
Vocabulary			

©2016 Hillary Wolfe, MA from *Writing Strategies for the Common Core*. This page may be reproduced for classroom use only.

Mini-lesson: Characteristics of Argument Text

Materials

- Chart paper
- Heavy card stock
- *Persuasive Strategy Cards* (one set of 6 cards per group), page 29
- *Situation Cards* (one set of 6 cards per group), page 30
- *Text Types and Purposes Chart* (optional), page 26

Overview

Students will be introduced to characteristics and types of argument text. They will continue to fill out the reference document to help them remember the characteristics and use the characteristics to help determine the types of argument writing.

Planning

Copy the *Situation Cards* template and *Persuasive Strategy Cards* template onto heavy card stock to create enough decks of cards so that each group of four students has six *Situation Cards* and six *Persuasive Strategy Cards*.

Procedure

Modeling

1. Introduce the vocabulary to the students that they will encounter in the lesson: *fact, data, sympathy, peer pressure.* Discuss examples of how these concepts are used as persuasive strategies (e.g., a fact demonstrates a provable reason, data provides evidence over time, sympathy relies on people responding to sad feelings, and power relies on response to a show of strength). Ask students to share with a partner some of their own examples. Write their ideas on chart paper, and post them in the front of the room.

2. Tell students they will be playing a game, and they will work in groups of four. The rules of the game are as follows:

   - A stack of six *Situation Cards* is placed facedown in the center of the table.
   - Each student is given one *Persuasive Strategy Card*. Place the remaining *Strategy Cards* facedown in the center of the table. A *Strategy Card* states the strategy on the front and offers a sentence starter on the back. (Take time to go over the descriptions to be sure that all students understand and have a chance to ask clarifying questions before the game begins.)
   - The game begins with one person as the judge. The judge turns over the top *Situation Card* for the group to read.
   - The *Situation Card* states the role that the judge will play and lists a situation that the other players are trying to argue for or against. For example, the *Situation Card* may say, "Audience = Friend. Convince your friend to join or leave a sport or game with you."
   - The judge for the round is the person that each player must "convince," but each player must use his or her strategy to do so. For example, a student with the strategy of "fact" might tell the judge, "It's a fact that people who play this sport are more likely to be injured."
   - Each student will have 30 seconds to use his or her strategy to convince the judge. After all students have tried, the judge will determine who was the most persuasive and award that player with the *Situation Card*.

3. All players hand their *Strategy Card* to the person on their right, and the role of the judge rotates one person to the right as well. The person who won the round places his or her *Strategy Card* in the center of the table and chooses a new *Strategy Card* from the deck.

4. Play continues until all players have had a chance to be the judge. The student who collected the most *Situation Cards* is the winner.

Guided Practice

5. Allow students between 15 and 20 minutes to complete the game. Walk around and facilitate as needed by answering questions about the strategies.

6. After the game is over, ask students to reflect with a partner on the game.

7. Tell students to take out their *Text Types and Purposes Charts*. In the first row of the second column, ask students what they think is the purpose of argument (to convince or persuade).

8. In the next row of the same column, have students write "strategy." Tell students that the strategies they used (sympathy, power play, fact, data, expert, peer pressure) are only a few of the ways authors try to be persuasive. Argument writing also relies on understanding your audience so you can choose the right tone and the appropriate language and words. Have students add "audience" and "word choice" in the "Features" row of their *Text Types and Purposes Chart*.

9. Have students add the vocabulary (sympathy, power play, fact, data) to the box in the third row.

Independent Practice

10. Have students write the answers to the following questions in their Reading Portfolios:

    a. Why did the role of the judge matter? (This speaks to audience, and how audience influences the tone and language of our persuasive argument.)

    b. Which types of persuasive strategies were most effective? Why do you think so?

    c. Which types of persuasive strategies were least effective? Why do you think so?

Optional extension: Ask students to look through magazines or newspapers or to find examples on television of different persuasive strategies. Have them bring in samples of what they find, and display them around the room.

Persuasive Strategy Cards (front)

Fact	Sympathy	Data
Peer Pressure	Expert	Power Play

Persuasive Strategy Cards (back)

"It is a **fact** that, _____, so _____."	"Isn't it **sad/painful** how _____."	"_____% of _____."
"All the popular people are _____."	"Doctors/scientists say, _____."	"I'm warning you, if you don't _____, then _____."

©2016 Hillary Wolfe, MA from *Writing Strategies for the Common Core*. This page may be reproduced for classroom use only.

Situation Cards

Role: Friend **Situation**: Join or quit a sport or game with you.	**Role**: Parent **Situation**: Get a snake as a pet.	**Role**: Older sibling **Situation**: Borrow a favorite piece of clothing or an electronic game.
Role: Younger sibling (or cousin) **Situation**: Go to bed.	**Role**: Neighbor **Situation**: Cut a low tree branch so you can skateboard on the sidewalk.	**Role**: Teacher **Situation**: Change your seat to sit next to your friend.

©2016 Hillary Wolfe, MA from *Writing Strategies for the Common Core*. This page may be reproduced for classroom use only.

Mini-lesson: Characteristics of Narrative Text

Materials

- Chart paper
- *Comic Book Hero!* activity sheet, page 33
- *Coming Soon!* activity sheet, page 34
- *Text Types and Purposes Chart* (optional), page 26

Overview

Students will be introduced to characteristics of narrative writing. They will complete their reference document to help them remember the characteristics and use the characteristics to help determine the purpose of narrative writing.

Planning

Make enough copies of the activity sheets for every student. Have samples of comics available to help students generate ideas about characters and to provide models of dialogue boxes, color choices, and page layouts. If students are having trouble thinking of a comic book hero, create some silly names and have students draw from a hat, or offer choices from categories, such as foods, animals, or geography. Choices could include "Pasta Boy/Girl" "Tiger Boy/Girl," or "Earthquake Boy/Girl."

Procedure

Modeling

1. Tell students that today they will be learning about the characteristics of narrative text. Explain that a narrative has a specific structure and contains specific features, just like the other genres they have worked with so far.
2. Introduce the vocabulary terms *story structure* and *character traits.*
3. Explain to students that one form of narrative writing is a comic book.
4. Ask students to brainstorm some of the features of a comic book. (Possible responses include a hero with specific powers, an archenemy, the story is told through picture boxes, dialogue.) Write students' ideas on chart paper and display in the front of the room.
5. Create categories that label the elements of a comic book: characters, setting, conflict.

Guided Practice

6. Distribute copies of the *Comic Book Hero!* activity sheets to students. Tell students they are to create an original story for a new comic book hero.
7. Have students fill in all the characteristics listed on the *Comic Book Hero!* activity sheet.
8. Ask students to share their page with one person in the class.
9. After all students have shared with a partner, each student will use the *Coming Soon!* activity sheet to describe their partner's character. The *Coming Soon!* activity sheet requires them to summarize the information as if it were a movie trailer. Students should be sure that their description includes information from each of the categories mentioned in step 5.
10. Have several students share their *Coming Soon!* activity sheet summaries.

Independent Practice

11. Ask students to take out their *Text Types and Purposes Chart.*

12. In the first row of the third column of the chart, have students write the purpose of a narrative. (Possible responses include: to tell a story or to relate a series of events.)

13. In the second row of the column, ask students to write the features of a narrative. (Possible responses include: characters, setting, conflict.)

14. Have students write the vocabulary words in the last row of the column. Explain that narratives have a specific story structure that includes a conflict that drives the story, and the characters have specific traits that ultimately help them resolve the conflict.

16. For a fun extension, have students use a narration website or app to narrate their trailer and share their narratives on the computer.

Characteristics of Narrative Text

Name: _____

Comic Book Hero!

Directions: Create a comic book hero using the form below. Fill out all the information about the character's traits, including his or her archenemy.

Draw a picture of your superhero:

Superpowers:

1. _____

2. _____

3. _____

Birthplace: _____

Sidekick: (optional) _____

Arch enemy: _____

How did the hero get his or her powers? _____

_____

©2016 Hillary Wolfe, MA from *Writing Strategies for the Common Core*. This page may be reproduced for classroom use only.

Characteristics of Narrative Text

Name: _____

Coming Soon!

Directions: Write a movie trailer about the comic book story presented to you by your partner. Include all elements of a narrative, including the character's traits, where he or she is from, and his or her arch enemy.

_____

_____

_____

_____

_____

_____

_____

_____

_____

_____

_____

_____

_____

_____

_____

    ©2016 Hillary Wolfe, MA from *Writing Strategies for the Common Core*. This page may be reproduced for classroom use only.

Overview: Writing from the Inside Out

When someone asks for directions to get somewhere, it's easier to provide them with a detailed map if you've actually made the trip yourself. You are able to quickly determine the important landmarks or road signs to watch for and can get your passenger to his or her destination as quickly as possible with minimal distractions. But if you've never been there yourself, all you can offer is a general idea of where to go, without really giving the kind of key information your traveler needs to be confident about the route.

The same is true for writing. When students try to write an essay by first focusing on the introduction, it's like trying to draw a map to a place they've never been. Yet that is what is asked of students all the time. They are expected to start with an introduction that describes their topic and then come up with a thesis—their opinion about the topic—including three or more reasons why they feel that way. Then they are to write their body paragraphs to support their thesis. This seems so backward! Imagine trying to make your route fit the map you drew!

Ideas don't occur in ready-made order. Students need to experience the stages of the writing process in which they brainstorm, put their ideas down, and then start to sort and organize them into some kind of order that makes sense. They could sort their ideas from most important to least important; or they could follow a sequential order. They could be writing to solve a problem, in which case they would want to explain the problem first and then offer several good solutions. In this case, they might want to save their best solution for last. Perhaps they are arguing for or against something. In this case, they may want to offer counterarguments along the way.

When students follow the steps of the writing process, they find that they are really writing from the inside out. They are putting their strongest ideas down on paper, then using strategies and tools to organize and sort those ideas. Then they can get feedback from others (peers or teachers) and revise their ideas, their organization, and even specific word choices. They may need to find more evidence to support their ideas, which may in turn influence their organization.

After students have spent some time manipulating their words and have settled on a structure, they will be ready to make their road map.

The introduction serves to tell the reader what he or she is about to encounter. It starts with a hook that invests the reader and then follows up with a description of what the reader can expect to find in the text. Then the introduction outlines the format and the key points of interest, so the reader knows what to look for and anticipates these transitions as he or she is reading.

If the student has already determined the structure and the key points, then writing the introduction is easy. The student only has to use his own paper as the reference document. But without this reference, the student is making it up and hoping the ideas that follow will actually match his introduction.

Step one is to help students determine how to distinguish relevant from unimportant details in a text. Once they know how to offer strong support for a main idea, they'll be on their way to creating an organized paper. Then, have students go back and write their introduction. Finally, have them write a closing that mirrors the introduction and sums up the journey that the reader took. The closing is almost like the memory book, offering souvenirs and mementos from the trip and reaffirming everything that was presented in the introduction.

You may have heard of this process before, described in this way:

- "Tell them what you're going to tell them."
- "Tell them."
- "Tell them what you told them."

Students may think this approach is a little strange at first, but ultimately it takes off a lot of pressure. They find that it is easier to throw out all kinds of ideas and then winnow them down to only their best thoughts. Then, when they write their introductions, they aren't overwhelmed by the prospect of what to write or how to start.

This section provides a Mini-lesson for identifying and writing main ideas and details. Then it introduces topic and concluding sentences as a way to provide structure to a paragraph. The last lesson gives students a chance to practice doing research so they understand the importance of using primary and secondary sources.

Mini-lesson: Main Ideas and Details

Materials

- Paper bag filled with random topics (see "Planning" section below for ideas)
- Red, green, and yellow (or any three colors) sticky notes or note cards (one set for each student)
- Chart paper
- Short nonfiction text passage
- *Main Ideas and Details* activity sheet, page 39
- *Text Types and Purposes Chart,* page 26

Overview

Students will identify and recognize significant details in nonfiction text and include significant details in their writing.

Planning

Before the lesson begins, write out a list of random topics, such as locations, television shows or movies, sports or recreational activities, famous people or events. Write one topic per slip of paper, and place all the slips in a paper bag for students to draw from. The topic they draw will be the topic they write their paragraph about.

Procedure

Modeling

1. Tell students that one of the problems many people have with writing is that they don't know what to say about their topic. Today students will learn a strategy for adding strong details to their writing.
2. Distribute three colored sticky notes or note cards to each student: one red, one green, and one yellow (or other colors you chose).
3. Tell students that there are three kinds of key details they can look for when they read: descriptions or definitions, causes and effects, or comparisons.
4. Have students explain *description* or *definition*. Ask students how they know when they are reading a description or a definition. What are some of the key clue words that alert them? Have students write "describe or define" on their red sticky note, and add a few of the clue words that they brainstormed.
5. To differentiate for language learners, ask students to come up with a hand motion or signal that represents *describe* or *define*. Practice the signal a few times while saying "describe or define."
6. Repeat steps 4 and 5 for "cause and effect," using the green sticky note and choosing a different hand motion.
7. Repeat steps 4 and 5 for "compare and contrast," using the yellow sticky note and choosing a different hand motion.

Guided Practice

8. Display a short passage of nonfiction text on the board and distribute copies to students. Ask students to read the passage silently while you read it aloud. Every time they hear one of the clue words that they wrote on their sticky notes, they should hold up that color sticky note.

9. Read a few lines together until you feel that students are correctly demonstrating understanding of the three types of details.

10. Have students work with partners or in groups of three or four. Give each group a sheet of chart paper. Ask them to continue reading the text. Each time they find a clue word, they should write the detail that they found on the appropriately colored sticky note (a definition on a red note, a cause and effect on a green note, and a comparison on a yellow note) and place it on the chart paper. Have each student write his or her initials on the sticky note for accountability. As you walk around, make sure all students have contributed at least one of each type of detail to the chart.

11. Have students share the charts showing the clues they identified.

12. Tell students that if they were able to recognize these details when they read, they should be able to add these kinds of details to their writing.

13. Model for students if necessary using a simple topic, such as cats or roller coasters. Display a large version of the *Main Ideas and Details* activity sheets and demonstrate how you add definitions or descriptions, causes and effects, and comparisons about the topic.

Independent Practice

14. Distribute the *Main Ideas and Details* activity sheets to students. Have each student draw one topic from the paper bag, and ask them to fill in the activity sheet about the topic.

15. Tell students this was a prewriting activity. After they have completed their activity sheets, they should keep it in their Reading and Writing Portfolios to use again in the next lesson.

16. Allow a few students to share their details. Then have students add detail types to the "features" row under the Explanatory column on their *Text Types and Purposes Chart*.

Extension

Revisit this activity, but add more types of details, such as a quote or a statistic.

If students struggle with...	Consider practicing these prerequisite skills:
recognizing definitions and descriptions	clues such as synonyms and antonyms, or cue words such as "for example"
recognizing causes and effects	clue words such as "since," "if...then," or "when...then"
recognizing comparisons	clue words such as "just like" or "different from"; Implicit comparisons, such as "more... most...all" or "some...others" or "better...best"

Main Ideas and Details

Name: _____

Directions: Use the graphic organizer below to choose a topic and come up with significant details about your topic.

Main Ideas and Details

Topic:
Define or describe your topic:
Name a cause or effect about your topic:
Compare or contrast your topic to something:

©2016 Hillary Wolfe, MA from *Writing Strategies for the Common Core*. This page may be reproduced for classroom use only.

Mini-lesson: Topic and Concluding Sentences

Materials

- Reading and Writing Portfolio
- Chart paper
- Colored card stock cut into sentence strips (5–7 strips per student)
- Colored paper for pockets
- Index cards
- Scissors
- Glue sticks
- *Main Ideas and Details* activity sheet (from previous lesson)
- *Topic and Concluding Sentences Graphic Organizer,* page 42

Overview

Students will assemble a paragraph by organizing their ideas using sentence strips; they will learn various ways to start a paragraph with an interesting topic sentence and then write a parallel sentence as a concluding statement. Students will collect interesting topic and concluding sentences and add them to their Reading and Writing Portfolios.

Planning

Have enough sentence strips available for every student to have five to seven each. Use one color for the topic and closing sentence strips, and a different color for the details sentence strips. Cut colored paper into squares that will fit into the Reading and Writing Portfolio.

Procedure

Modeling

1. Have students refer to their *Main Ideas and Details* activity sheets. Review the types of details students used to describe their topics: definitions and descriptions, causes and effects, and comparisons. Have students circle or highlight the topic, as they will use this same topic for the following activity.

2. Distribute copies of the *Topic and Concluding Sentences Graphic Organizer* to students. In the top left box, ask students to write their topic from the previous lesson.

3. Have students look at Box 1, "Proper Noun." On chart paper, ask students to help you co-construct a definition of a proper noun. Have students brainstorm examples of proper nouns and then write the definition of a proper noun in their own words on their graphic organizers. Ask students to write a topic sentence about their topic that starts with a proper noun.

4. Have students look at Box 2, "Verb." On chart paper, ask students to help you co-construct a definition of a verb. Have students brainstorm examples of verbs, and then write the definition in their own words on their graphic organizers. Ask students to write a sentence about their topic that starts with a verb.

5. Repeat step 3 for Box 3, "Adjective."

6. Tell students to refer to the *Main Ideas and Details* activity sheet. Have them write each of their detail sentences, one per sentence strip.

7. Give students a few minutes to organize their detail sentences by moving their sentences around. Ask students to try different orders until they find the one that they think makes the most sense. Ask students to explain their choice on the graphic organizer.

8. Tell them to choose one sentence from the graphic organizer to be their topic sentence and to write that sentence on one of the two remaining sentence strips. Have them place this strip above the details.

9. Ask students to evaluate if their paragraph makes sense by turning to a partner to read aloud. Students may decide to reorder their sentences after discussion with a peer.

10. When students are pleased with their paragraphs, tell them they still need a concluding sentence. The concluding sentence must match the topic sentence. For example, if the topic sentence started with a verb, then the concluding sentence should also start with a verb. The verb should be a synonym of the first verb. In other words, the concluding sentence should not be the same sentence as the topic. Help students restate the topic sentence, not repeat it using Box 4.

Independent Practice

11. Give students time to write out their paragraphs, either on paper or using a computer.

12. Have students glue two colored squares into their Reading and Writing Portfolios to serve as pockets. Tell them to label one pocket "Topic Sentences" and the other pocket "Concluding Sentences."

13. Have students interview at least three other peers and copy their topic and concluding sentences onto index cards. Have them circle and identify whether the sentence started with proper nouns, verbs, or adjectives. Ask students to keep the sentences in the pockets.

14. Tell students that as they read nonfiction text, they can collect interesting topic sentences and concluding sentences and write them on index cards to keep in the pockets. Encourage them to circle and identify the first words of these sentences. These will serve as references for future writing projects.

Extension

Post interesting topic and concluding sentences on a poster in the room, and encourage students to add sentences to the class collection. Students can use any sentence from the class collection or their own collections as model topic and concluding sentences when they write.

Formative Assessment

If students struggle with...	Consider practicing these prerequisite skills:
recognizing verbs, proper nouns, adjectives	parts of speech, grammar rules, and language conventions

Topic and Concluding Sentences

Name: _____

Topic and Concluding Sentences Graphic Organizer

Topic My topic is	**Box 1** A proper noun is _____ _____ Write a sentence about your topic that starts with a proper noun: _____ _____ _____
Box 2 A verb is _____ _____ Write a sentence about your topic that starts with a verb: _____ _____ _____	**Box 3** An adjective is _____ _____ Write a sentence about your topic that starts with an adjective: _____ _____ _____

Box 4

Write a concluding sentence that sums up your ideas

_____

_____

 ©2016 Hillary Wolfe, MA from *Writing Strategies for the Common Core*. This page may be reproduced for classroom use only.

Chapter 2

Response to Literature

Overview: Understanding Text Types and Purposes

The anchor standards for writing outlined in the Common Core State Standards describe a set of standards categorized as "Research to Build and Present Knowledge." This category includes the specific standard: "Draw evidence from literary or informational texts to support analysis, reflection, and research." The implication for students is that they have a deep comprehension of the text they are reading and that they can pick out the specific details in the text that inform their analysis.

The connection to reading is evident in the expectations. Students must be able to read closely to find the significant details they will use as evidence. Many students, and struggling readers in particular, have trouble understanding exactly what is meant by a "significant detail." When they read, everything is given equal weight, and distinguishing what is important from what is superfluous can be challenging. The lessons in this section define the types of significant details students should look for specific to each text type. By providing an identifying label, students can read more purposefully because they are looking for very specific clue words that will alert them when a line is important. Once they find it in their reading, they can discuss it with authority in their writing. This type of analysis is excellent practice for writing original works, because students will have had exposure to the use of very explicit ways to support a main idea. When it is their turn to write in a specific text type, they can be reminded of mentor texts they have read that have served as models.

Reading Strategy: Responding to Explanatory/Informational Text

In grades three through five, children begin to read in order to access information and learn from text. They learn to identify key details, summarize ideas, and make inferences. Students are able to recognize text structures and to grapple with why an author makes specific choices. These skills will eventually allow students to engage in deeper textual analyses about underlying themes and generalizable ideas. Young students who struggle with reading can certainly learn how to identify a text structure, but to understand why the author made that choice will take practice. Learning how to make specific choices as writers themselves will help students practice engaging with text from a new perspective.

The continued and prevalent use of high-stakes writing tests demonstrates the need for effective responses to literature. Regardless of genre, students need tools to help them perform close readings under a tight time constraint. They will need tools that will help them discern the significance of elements and then transfer that analysis skill across multiple platforms.

Close reading means that students purposefully examine text. They need practice looking at all the elements of text, from organization and text structure to specific features of text, such as headings, diagrams, photos, and captions. Secondary teachers assume that students learned how their textbooks functioned in earlier grades. The elementary teacher is responsible for highlighting and explicitly teaching the structures of literary and nonfiction texts. In addition, technology has changed the way students take in information (holistically versus sequentially). Students need skills and strategies to access complex reading materials.

Focus: Supporting Details

Once they identify the text features and understand their functions, students are on their way to understanding the many types of details that authors rely upon to support their ideas. Responding to explanatory and informational text allows students an opportunity to evaluate the effectiveness of different types of supporting details, which can lead to them making more informed choices about the kinds of details they use to support their own ideas when they write.

The Mini-lesson shows students several different types of evidence that are appropriate to supporting a main idea in an explanatory or informational text. They will define these details and practice identifying them by using specific clue words. Then, students will demonstrate their understanding by writing a statement that shows they recognize the type of detail and the purpose that it serves.

Mini-lesson: Text Features and Significant Details

Materials

- Sample textbooks, cookbooks, reference materials, or websites (one per student)
- *Text Features Graphic Organizer,* page 47
- *Connecting Reading to Writing Chart,* page 48
- *Reading Strategy Game Cards* (one set per group of 4 students), pages 49–50
- *Reading Strategy Game Tally Sheet* (one per group of 4 students), page 51

Overview

Students will be introduced to different text features and analyze each feature's purpose. They will also be introduced to six types of significant details that are often used to support main ideas in explanatory text. Students will complete a graphic organizer to use as a reference for different text features and types of significant details.

Planning

Many types of books can be used for this lesson. Use content-area textbooks, or print a page from of a popular website to use as an example. The page chosen for display should have several text features represented, such as charts, maps, diagrams, several different fonts, headings, photos or illustrations with captions, tables, and so on. Try to choose text that has as many different features represented as possible.

Procedure

Modeling

1. Tell students that they will be learning about text features and types of significant details that most commonly appear in informational text. Distribute copies of the *Text Features Graphic Organizer* to each student. Give each student one textbook or reference text.

2. Display a sample page from a textbook, or use a page from a website. Display the page either through a computer-based projector or a document camera.

   Post a sheet of chart paper and draw a three-column chart. Label the columns as follows: "Feature," "What It Is," "What It Does." Have students refer to the chart on their graphic organizers.

3. Ask students to call out some of the features they notice about the displayed text. Students should notice fonts, headings, sidebars, photos, diagrams, captions, tables, tabs, and so on. Chart students' answers in the "Feature" column on the chart paper.

4. Choose one feature, such as headings. Ask students to describe a heading. Answers may include: words that are larger than the paragraph, words in bold, words set off by two line spaces. Chart student answers in the "What It Is" column. Have students write on their graphic organizers.

5. Ask students to explain the purpose of a heading. Think aloud to help students understand that a heading can serve as a title, a mini-summary, or a description of the main idea of the text that follows. Chart their answers in the "What It Does" column as students write on their own sheets.

Guided Practice

6. Have students work with partners to choose two or more features each and add them to their graphic organizers. Ask students to display or share out their organizers for comment by other students.

7. Have students refer to the *Connecting Reading to Writing Chart*. Explain to students that when they read explanatory text, they use specific reading strategies. Point to the left side of the chart, and identify *visualize, predict, connect, question, infer,* and *summarize.*

8. Point to the right side of the chart, and explain how authors help readers use those strategies: by adding *descriptive details*, the reader can *visualize*; by adding *causes and effects*, the reader can *predict*; by adding *comparisons*, the reader can *connect*; by adding *interesting and unusual facts*, the reader can *question*; by adding *personal examples*, the reader can *infer*; and by using a *specific structure*, the reader can *summarize.*

9. Have students read the examples on the chart with a partner. Ask students to discuss and share out how the examples are indicative of the author's use of a strategy.

Independent Practice

10. Ask students to work in groups of four. Distribute copies of the *Reading Strategy Game Cards* and *Reading Strategy Game Tally Sheet* to students.

11. Explain that they will take turns pulling a card and deciding which type of reading strategy is represented on the card. Students will rotate playing the role of the judge, who will choose the card and give the correct answer for that round.

12. After each round, the role of the judge rotates one person to the left. The judge will record on the tally sheet the number of correct responses for each student.

13. For an extra point, the students who get the correct answer can create a new example, and the rest of the students must judge whether it represents the strategy accurately.

14. After the game, have students write an explanation in their own words of each type of detail they examined and its purpose in informational text.

Text Features and Significant Details

Name: _____

Text Features Graphic Organizer

Directions: Fill in the chart below with features you can find in your text. Describe each feature in the What It Is column, and explain the purpose of that feature in the What It Does column.

Feature	What It Is	What It Does
heading	words that are larger than the paragraph, words in bold, words set off by two line spaces	title, a mini-summary, or a description of the main idea of the text that follows

©2016 Hillary Wolfe, MA from *Writing Strategies for the Common Core*. This page may be reproduced for classroom use only.

Connecting Reading to Writing Chart

For a reader to:	The writer must:
Visualize	**Use descriptive words** Ex.: The crystal blue waters of the lake were calm and still until a gentle breeze created a soft ripple on the surface.
Predict	**Show clear causes and effects** Ex.: Exercise may be hard at first, but keep at it. Eventually you will build up endurance.
Connect	**Make comparisons** Ex.: Don't be too quick to judge. Remember the story of the ugly duckling? You never know when a swan will show itself.
Question	**Provide interesting and unusual facts** Ex.: There are many dangerous animals in Australia.
Infer	**Use relatable or personal examples** Ex.: Being born a stray, the dog was a survivor. His new owner tried to remember that as he searched the streets for his missing pet.
Summarize	**Organize information logically** Ex.: There are three important reasons why bullying is wrong.

 ©2016 Hillary Wolfe, MA from *Writing Strategies for the Common Core*. This page may be reproduced for classroom use only.

Reading Strategy Game Cards

The map shows a picture of a man in a bed. That means "hotel." *Visualize*	A polar bear lives in a very challenging habitat. He makes his home among white ice, freezing rain, and dark skies. *Visualize*	Some people laughed at Christopher Columbus. They were sure his ships would slide off the edge of the earth. But Columbus was sure his trip would work. *Predict*
What do you think will happen if you add baking soda to vinegar? *Predict*	The first man in space was an explorer, just like Magellan. He was heading off into a great unknown. *Connect*	To picture a fraction, think about a download bar on the computer. As the image loads, only a fraction (or portion) of it is ready for viewing. *Connect*

©2016 Hillary Wolfe, MA from *Writing Strategies for the Common Core*. This page may be reproduced for classroom use only.

Reading Strategy Game Cards

The longest python found was 10 feet, but later the size was adjusted to 11 feet. The adjustment was made because it is difficult to measure a python. *Question*	The water cycle is also responsible for changes in the geography of the earth. *Question*	Yesterday, the boys didn't sell one glass of lemonade at their stand. Today the temperature outside is 10 degrees higher. They work quickly to make a double batch. *Infer*
The girl didn't say anything when her toy was stolen. She just sat quietly, but her cheeks turned red and her breathing became louder. *Infer*	The bus route includes several stops along the way. Each stop has a landmark. You will come to three landmarks before reaching your stop. *Summarize*	Read the table of contents to locate the chapter, or use the index to find a specific topic. *Summarize*

 ©2016 Hillary Wolfe, MA from *Writing Strategies for the Common Core*. This page may be reproduced for classroom use only.

Reading Strategy Card Game Tally Sheet

Directions: Write the name of each player in the top row. Keep track of each time that player correctly identifies the reading strategy associated with the sentence. Award an extra point if the player can correctly invent a similar example.

©2016 Hillary Wolfe, MA from *Writing Strategies for the Common Core*. This page may be reproduced for classroom use only.

Reading Strategy: Responding to Argument Text

Argument text refers to the ability to state a claim and back it up with evidence. Students will likely encounter argument text without even realizing it, through ads, billboards, and packaging. The writing anchor standards indicate that students should be able to "gather relevant information from multiple print and digital sources" and "assess the credibility and accuracy of each source." To be college and career ready for the 21st century, the definition of text must be expanded to include these various formats. Writing is the vehicle that allows students to express the connections between these media. Through writing, students can discuss content in whatever format it may take.

Focus: Types of Appeals

To be critical thinkers, students need practice determining if information is credible and accurate. Modern writing makes use of multiple persuasive techniques, including visual elements, sound, and music, along with strong word choices and humor. Students need to be well-versed in identifying each of these elements so they can view the message as a whole with objectivity and with bias, if not eliminated, at least acknowledged.

This lesson highlights the different ways that an author can be persuasive and asks students to determine the credibility of that technique in light of the purpose of the text as well as the intended audience. When students can be made aware of these factors, they can read text with a critical eye and be more cognizant of their responses. Then students can authoritatively state that they understand why an author chose a particular type of appeal and evaluate the effect of that appeal.

Mini-lesson: How Appealing!

Materials

- Chart paper
- Notebook paper
- *Supporting Statements Chart,* pages 55–56
- *Support That Topic! Worksheet,* pages 57–58
- *Topic Cards* (one set per group of 3 students), page 59
- *Fact/Example Die Net* (one die per group), page 60
- *Blank Die Net,* page 61
- *Transition Words Die Net* (one die per group), page 62

Overview

Students will practice supporting an opinion with facts and personal examples. Students will start experimenting with a problem-solution text structure to frame their opinions.

Planning

The dice for the game can be made ahead of time by using the nets provided. A blank net has also been included so students can come up with their own examples to play the game on different occasions. Copy and cut the *Topic Cards* so that each group has one set.

Procedure

Modeling

1. Tell students that an argument means to present an opinion and then use facts and personal examples to support that opinion. Authors choose different combinations of facts and personal examples and use specific structures to present their argument in a logical way. Authors make these choices based upon the purpose of the argument and the audience to whom the argument is addressed.

2. Distribute copies of the *Supporting Statements Chart* to students and help them identify how these types of support are similar and how they are different. Have students sort the statements into the "Facts" or "Personal Examples" columns.

Guided Practice

3. Check for understanding and have students share their answers with a partner and then with the class.

4. Distribute copies of the *Support That Topic! Worksheet.* Model for students how to fill in the chart by writing either a fact or a personal example for each topic offered. Challenge students to think of additional topics they could write about and write their ideas in the blank spaces.

5. Ask students which type of support is easier to write. Why? Have students share their answers with a partner. Which supporting statements were the most effective? Tell students to place a check mark by any statements they especially liked.

6. Have students refer to the sentence frame on the next page of the worksheet. Explain how opinion writing often uses a problem-solution structure (show them the example on the worksheet). Point out the use of transition words that link the ideas together (*because, one thing, an example*). Brainstorm other transition words and chart them on the board or a sheet of poster paper.

7. Have students work with a partner and practice using the frame to state their opinions about the topics mentioned earlier. Students may use the frame as is or create their own version that states a problem and offers a solution.

Independent Practice

8. Have students work in groups of three. Give each group one set of *Topic Cards*, one *Fact/Example Die Net*, and one *Transition Words Die Net*. Explain the rules of the game: One person will choose a *Topic Card* and roll the dice. The other two students will then have two minutes to silently write a problem-solution sentence using either a fact or an example (whichever was rolled) and the transition word that was rolled. After two minutes, students turn their sentences over to the judge, who will rate the statements. The person whose statement seems the most effective will win the round, and the role of the judge will rotate to another player.

9. After all students have had a chance to be judge at least twice, ask students to take out a sheet of notebook paper and write an explanation in their own words on the following topic: *Describe three things that you should include when you write an opinion.* Assess students' use of the academic vocabulary as they describe opinion writing.

Formative Assessment

If students struggle with...	Consider practicing these prerequisite skills:
facts	characteristics of a fact, such as "can be proven" or "often includes data"
personal examples and opinions	characteristics of an opinion, such as "not everyone agrees" or "isn't always true"

How Appealing!

Name: _____

Supporting Statements Chart

Directions: Sort the statements below into the appropriate columns. The first two have been done for you.

1. ~~When parks are well lit, it is safer for kids to play.~~

2. ~~One time I was at the park when it was dark and I didn't see a construction sign saying, "Stay out!"~~

3. Dogs have been pets for humans for thousands of years.

4. My dog is so smart he can catch popcorn in his mouth!

5. A bully is someone who threatens you, either physically or emotionally.

6. Bullies are often people who have been bullied themselves.

7. My sister stood up to a bully once and the bullying stopped.

8. The class field trip to the zoo showed us how important it is to treat animals kindly.

9. Animals live longer when they are treated well and live in a safe environment.

Facts	Personal Examples
When parks are well lit, it is safer for kids to play.	One time I was at the park when it was dark and I didn't see a construction sign saying, "Stay out!"

©2016 Hillary Wolfe, MA from *Writing Strategies for the Common Core*. This page may be reproduced for classroom use only.

Facts	Personal Examples

©2016 Hillary Wolfe, MA from *Writing Strategies for the Common Core*. This page may be reproduced for classroom use only.

How Appealing!

Support That Topic! Worksheet

Directions: Read the topics and consider your opinion on each topic. Write one fact or one personal example to support your opinion.

Topic	Fact	Personal Example
Video games: good or bad?		
Recycling helps our environment.		
Show more movies in school.		
Give up summer vacation for year-round school.		
Kids should get more exercise.		
Outlaw soda for kids under 16.		

©2016 Hillary Wolfe, MA from *Writing Strategies for the Common Core*. This page may be reproduced for classroom use only.

Problem-Solution Sentence Frame

One problem that many people face is _____

_____.

(topic)

This is a problem because _____

_____.

(your opinion of the topic)

But we can solve this problem. One thing we can do is _____

_____.

(a solution, based on a fact)

An example of how this would help is _____

_____.

(a personal example that supports your opinion)

©2016 Hillary Wolfe, MA from *Writing Strategies for the Common Core*. This page may be reproduced for classroom use only.

Topic Cards

Build a skate park at school	Ban chocolate milk at school	Students should wear school uniforms
Limit video games at home	Take P.E. out of school	Let kids take online classes
Fine people who don't recycle	Clean up the water supply	Reward bystanders who see bullying and try to help

©2016 Hillary Wolfe, MA from *Writing Strategies for the Common Core*. This page may be reproduced for classroom use only.

Fact/Example Die Net

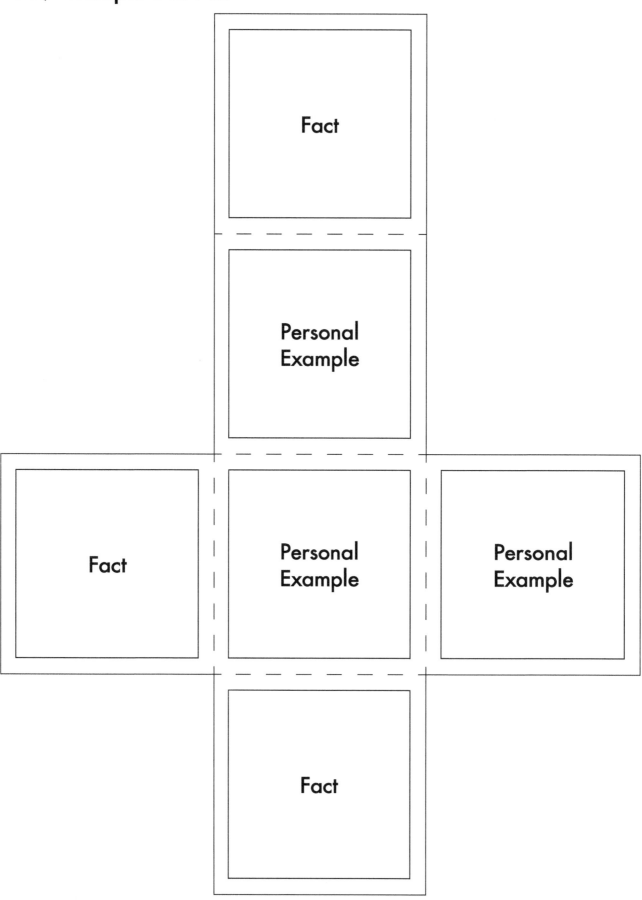

©2016 Hillary Wolfe, MA from *Writing Strategies for the Common Core*. This page may be reproduced for classroom use only.

Blank Die Net

©2016 Hillary Wolfe, MA from *Writing Strategies for the Common Core*. This page may be reproduced for classroom use only.

Transition Words Die Net

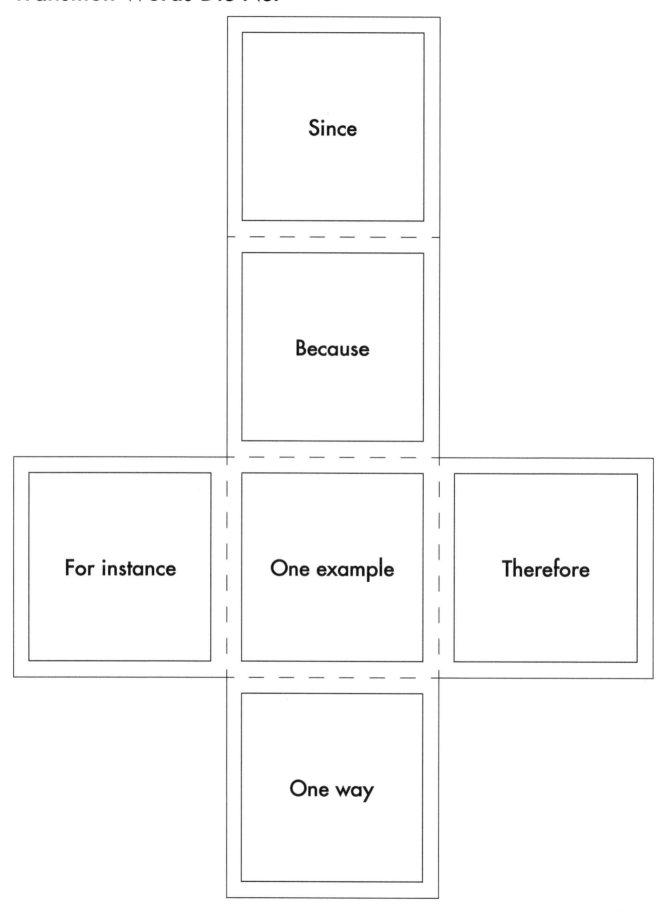

Since

Because

For instance

One example

Therefore

One way

©2016 Hillary Wolfe, MA from *Writing Strategies for the Common Core*. This page may be reproduced for classroom use only.

Reading Strategy: Responding to Narrative Text

It may seem that responding to narrative text is easy. We naturally seem to relate to a narrative since it represents a story or sequence of events, and we are more practiced in this conventional writing form. But it is just as important for students to recognize what they are responding to when they encounter a narrative. Are they connecting to the character's situation? To the character's feelings? To the challenge the character faced? Once students can identify why the text has had an impact on them, they can more easily identify the theme of the story and how that theme comes from the lesson or moral of the tale.

Focus: Language and Word Choice

Although many students don't believe it, authors make very deliberate word choices when they write. Reading a text is like having a one-sided conversation with the author. If the student were face-to-face with the author, the student would have the benefit of seeing the author's expressions, hearing the intonations in his or her voice, and understanding the subtle body language that conveys emotions and tone. In the one-sided conversation that we have as readers, though, the author understands that the only way to convey emotion and tone is through devices, such as dialogue, sensory descriptions, and specific sequences of events.

This lesson allows students to experiment with different literary techniques to see the emotional impact that each one can have. Then students will realize that as a narrative writer, they have many tools at their disposal to add emotional punch to their own writing.

Mini-lesson: Literary Devices

Materials

- Samples of short narrative texts
- *Literary Devices Chart* (one to distribute and one to display), pages 66–67
- *Predict the Lesson or Moral* activity sheet, page 68

Overview

Students will examine the different types of literary devices and see how each device can be used to support a theme.

Planning

Choose short narrative pieces that students can read quickly with partners. Be sure to enforce the correct use of academic language and terminology, and ask students to respond in complete sentences.

Procedure

Modeling

1. Tell students that a narrative is a story or sequence of events, but it could take the form of a poem, a song, a fictional story, a biography, a diary, or a news story. Explain that the purpose of a narrative is to get the reader to understand some important lesson or idea so that the story can help the reader make choices in his or her own life.

2. Distribute the *Literary Devices Chart* to students. Introduce the terminology in the chart, and use examples from different texts to demonstrate how each device may appear in a narrative. Check for understanding and have students work with partners to explain their understanding of each device in their own words.

Guided Practice

3. Display a sample of a short narrative text, or distribute copies of the text to partners. Have students read the text and use the *Literary Devices Chart* to identify the various literary devices. Have them use the sentence frame on the *Process Steps* sheet as a model to express their responses.

4. Distribute the *Predict the Lesson or Moral* activity sheets to students. Use a sample narrative to think aloud how you fill in the chart. Complete the first one for students, then do a second example with student partners discussing their answers and sharing out.

Independent Practice

5. Distribute a new narrative text. Have students read the text and use the *Literary Devices Chart* and the *Predict the Lesson or Moral* activity sheets to respond to the various devices.

6. Ask students to write a one-paragraph response to the text in which they identify the theme and explain how at least two literary devices support that theme.

Optional: Have students use a software program to write and animate a story online. Have them explain the choices they made about the way the characters looked and dressed and about the setting they chose.

Formative Assessment

If students struggle with...	Consider practicing these prerequisite skills:
setting	sensory descriptions
character traits	dialogue, point of view, narration
conflict	problem and solution structures

Literary Devices Chart

Literary Device	Definition	Purpose	Example(s)	Implication
Setting	Where and when the story takes place	Provides context and situations for the characters	• The summer of the year 1845 in New Orleans • A dark and stormy night • Inside the brightly lit grounds of an amusement park	• Hot and humid, southern U.S. before the Civil War • Scary, threatening • Fun, happy, kid-friendly
Character traits	The way a character acts, thinks, or speaks that reveals his or her personality	To understand why the character makes certain choices in the story	• "She lowered her eyes and swallowed her anger." • "He threw his head back and laughed." • "The dog wagged its tail and leapt for joy."	• She doesn't stand up for herself. • He is a happy and fun person. • The dog loves his life.
Conflict	A challenge that must be overcome or a quest that must be fulfilled	To highlight how the character changes and grows over time or how the character learns a lesson	• The character wants to be stronger, so he takes a magic potion. • The character is lost and must find her way home. • Something has been taken from the character, and he needs to get it back.	• He learns that real strength comes from within. • She realizes that she can take care of herself. • He learns to value the things he has.

 ©2016 Hillary Wolfe, MA from *Writing Strategies for the Common Core*. This page may be reproduced for classroom use only.

Process Steps

1. Read the passage.

2. Identify the setting, character traits, and the conflict.

3. Ask yourself: What are the implications of each element? (Use the chart to help you.)

4. Explain your answer using the sentence frame below.

In this story, the setting is _____

_____.

The author chose this setting because _____

_____.

The main character's personality is _____

_____.

This is shown in the way the character says/behaves/thinks _____

_____

_____.

In this story, the conflict is _____

_____

_____.

Literary Devices

Name: _____

Predict the Lesson or Moral

Directions: Read a short narrative, and fill in the chart below. Then determine the moral.

Describe the setting:	Cite an example from the text:	This makes me think of:
Describe the character(s):	Cite an example from the text:	This makes me think of:
Describe the conflict:	Cite an example from the text:	This makes me think of:

I think the moral is: _____

_____

_____.

©2016 Hillary Wolfe, MA from *Writing Strategies for the Common Core*. This page may be reproduced for classroom use only.

Chapter 3

Explanatory and Informational Text

Overview of the Genre

Purpose

Explanatory and informational text does just what it says: It explains something. In the last section, students were introduced to this genre and discovered that there are three main purposes for writing in this style:

- To explain *how* something works (a process)
- To explain *why* something works (a cause and effect)
- To explain a *relationship* (a comparison)

Each type of explanatory text shares similar components, which will help students recognize this kind of writing when they read and also help them include these components as writers. The common elements are what will help strengthen the reading and writing connection.

Audience

Understanding audience helps students make informed choices about the structure and language to use when they write. When reading informational text, students should ask themselves, "Who was this written for?" Help them notice the word choices and the structure, and have them think about who the text appeals to. For example, a city guide book for kids will look different and use different language than if it were written for adults. When they write, students should be reminded to think of who their intended audience is and use that information to make language and structure choices too.

In order to understand intended audience, it will be important for students to have reading put into a context, either historically or topically, in order to make it relevant. Pre-teach any important historical facts and scientific or mathematical principles that are necessary to achieve a true understanding of the text.

Reading Strategy: Predicting

Focus: Text Structure

The first thing students must recognize is the structure of an explanatory text. The strong organizational style of explanatory text will help students as they read because they can better predict what will come next and how to find main ideas and details when they understand the consistent structure. Some structures include step by step, which outlines in sequential order a procedure or task. A chronological structure presents an explanation in terms of time, describing a series of events as they occur over a specific span, such as a timeline (large scale) or a recipe (think of baking bread). A cause-and-effect structure offers a description of an event and then explains the circumstances that led to that event or describes an event and explains the consequences of that event. A compare-and-contrast structure will describe one facet or situation first, then describe the contrasting facet or situation next, and may end with a paragraph that sums up; or the first paragraph may offer all the ways two things are similar, and the next paragraph might demonstrate all the ways they are different.

Focus: Transition Words

Being able to recognize transition words will help students determine or predict which type of explanatory text they are reading. Typically, a step-by-step or chronological text will use sequential transitions, such as *first, next, then*, and *finally*, since it is describing a process or procedure. A cause-and-effect text will use transitions such as *when, then, as a result*, and *after.* A comparison text will use transitions that show similarities and differences, such as *similar to, as opposed to, however*, and *just like.* When students recognize the structure of text and recognize the transition words, they can more easily identify that they are reading an explanatory text, and by determining which type of explanatory text they are reading, they can make a prediction about what will follow.

When students write, they can choose key structures and transition words to match their topic. Because they have practiced finding these words in reading and recognizing the specific uses for each type of structure and transition word, students can narrow down their word choices to align to the type of text they themselves are composing.

Reading Strategy: Visualizing

Focus: Descriptive and Sensory Words

One comprehension strategy we ask students to use is visualizing. We want them picturing what they read so they can create mental images. This helps students hold on to the words because they can "see" what is happening. To be able to visualize, students need to find those places in the text that are particularly descriptive. Have them look specifically for sensory words. These will anchor their ability to visualize what they are reading. The more senses involved, the stronger the picture will be.

As writers, then, students need to practice adding strong sensory details. Students should be as vivid as they can when describing how something looks, feels, tastes, smells, and so on. The more vivid they can be in their descriptions, the better their reader will understand what they're trying to say.

Sometimes the words will not be enough, and the text may include a graphic—a picture, illustration, or chart—to provide additional details to help explain. Students should be reminded that these visual elements are not included just to take up space. Sometimes the picture or chart is more descriptive than any words could be.

Focus: Word Choice

In addition to sensory descriptions, authors choose very specific terms because of the many shades of meaning associated with them. The sentence, "The table was made of wood," is not nearly as descriptive as "The dining table was made of caramel-colored chestnut." The second sentence clarifies what kind of table, as well as what kind of wood, and then describes the color of the wood to add even more dimension to the description. The second sentence is definitely easier to picture than the first.

As writers, students need to practice revising their work to look for places where they were vague or ambiguous and tighten up their writing by adding specific adjectives, explicit nouns, and more interesting verbs that will deepen the reader's awareness and understanding of the topic.

Prerequisite Skills

Because this unit will focus on the reading strategies of summarizing, using text structures, and visualizing, students will need practice with these tools. Provide Mini-lessons on specific adjectives, explicit nouns, and active verbs so students have a store of words from which to choose when it comes time for them to do their own writing. Expose students to texts that utilize different text structures, and have students practice identifying the transition words. Use summarizing strategies repeatedly, and have students practice them with short pieces of text as well as long pieces.

Specific Content-area Vocabulary

If students will be writing in a specific content area, front load the vocabulary they will need so they are familiar with it and can use it comfortably. There are a number of strategies for introducing and practicing vocabulary and for creating and maintaining a word-conscious environment in your classroom so that vocabulary use is authentically woven into daily instruction. Create word walls, give points or rewards each time students use a vocabulary word in natural conversation, or encourage them to use Frayer Models or other concept-mapping tools so they make strong connections to words.

During reading, students may still encounter unknown words, so it is important to teach them decoding strategies as well. Some decoding strategies they can use during reading include:

- Looking at the context to determine what the word probably means.
- Seeing if the word is defined in the text by an example or a non-example.
- Looking at the root words and try to cipher out the meaning.
- Determining the part of speech to help understand how the word is being used.

Sample Planning Calendar

Monday	Tuesday	Wednesday	Thursday	Friday
RI: Visualization	RP: Visualization	WI: Observations	WP: Observations	RP/WP: Visualization Observations
RI: Text structures	RI: Predicting	RP: Text structures WI: Processes	RP: Predicting WI: Processes	RP: Text structures V: Transitional words
RI: Main ideas and details	RP: Main ideas and details WI: Supporting details	WP: Supporting details WI: Openings Closings	RI: Word choice WI: Compound sentences G: Verbs, adverbs, adjectives	WP: Drafting
WP: Revising	RP: Comprehension check	WP: Editing G: Complex sentences and conjunctions TEST PREP	TEST PREP	TEST PREP

Legend

RI = Reading Instruction
RP = Reading Practice
WI = Writing Instruction
WP = Writing Practice
V = Vocabulary
G = Grammar

Strategy Overview: Sensory and Descriptive Writing

For many students, the idea of writing seems daunting. If they haven't had a lot of practice, students may lack confidence and may feel like writing is a skill they are lacking.

These students need to see that writing is indeed a process, and that when they break it down into tiny steps, it becomes more manageable and less scary. Instead of focusing on *everything* they want to say, start small by focusing on one thing at a time. Begin by emphasizing what students *can* do, and add in challenges gradually. And above all else, make writing engaging and fun so that students have a real-life experience to hang on to. This will enhance their descriptions and their writing.

In this section, students will practice sensory and descriptive writing by making observations that use all their senses. They will also describe a process using as many descriptive terms as they can to be explicit and detailed. Through guided prewriting activities, students will see how they can add rich dimension to their words and expand their writing even further.

Use these lessons during the prewriting stage of the writing process to get students in a frame of mind for writing and to fill their word banks with rich and varied word choices.

Prewriting Mini-lesson: Observations

Materials

- Stuffed animal or other engaging object
- Chart paper
- Small timers (hourglasses) set for one-minute intervals (one per group of 4 students)
- Lemons, oranges, or some other fruit, cut in half and placed in a plastic bag (one bag per group of 4 students)
- Reading and Writing Portfolio
- *Sense It Activity Cards* (one set per group of 4 students), page 76
- *Sense It Activity Spinner* (one per group of 4 students), page 77
- *Text Types and Purposes Chart,* page 26

Overview

Students will practice using sensory details to describe a piece of fruit.

Planning

Before the lesson begins, cut the fruit in half and place the halved pieces in each plastic bag. This lesson can be used as part of a culminating assignment in which students make repeated observations and then write an explanatory essay about the decomposition of the fruit. Additional templates are included to complete the culminating assignment.

Procedure

Modeling

1. Hold up a stuffed animal. Ask students to describe it without naming it.
2. Label one sheet of chart paper "See." Ask students to describe what they see. Write down all their ideas, including colors, shapes, size, and so on.
3. Label another sheet of chart paper "Feel." Have a few students touch the toy and describe how it feels. Give them some words to help, such as *fuzzy, soft, squishy, floppy.*
4. Ask students to tell you some other ways they could describe the toy. (Possible responses include *how it smells, how it moves.*) Chart their ideas on a third sheet of paper.

Guided Practice

5. Ask students to work in groups of four. Distribute a set of *Sense It Activity Cards, a Sense It Activity Spinner,* and a timer to each group.
6. Tell students how to play the game. Student groups split into two teams. For the first round, one person draws a card and holds it faceup on his or her forehead (so the partner can see it). The partner then spins the spinner, which determines how the topic on the card may be described. The partner has one minute to get his or her teammate to guess as many of the topics as possible, using only one type of sensory description. Once the time is up, the other team spins and draws and competes to get more answers correct than the first team.

7. Have students share their experiences. Which descriptions were easier to state? Sight or touch? Which senses were the most difficult to describe?

8. Ask students to share out some of their most successful descriptions. Why were those easy to visualize? Ask students to rank the senses from most to least descriptive.

9. Tell students to add information to their *Text Types and Purposes Chart* to describes the kind of language used in explanatory text.

10. Have students write I-spy riddles about an object in the classroom. Collect student riddles and periodically read them aloud for the class to try and guess. Award extra credit points for particularly inventive descriptions.

Reading Connection

Give students sticky notes or bookmarks with a symbol on it that represents visualizing. Give students a piece of text, and have them place their sticky note or bookmark each time they visualized what they read. Model this for students using a piece of descriptive writing.

Next, have students go back to the places they marked in the text, and ask them to circle or highlight the exact word or words that helped them form a picture in their minds. Ask students to determine how many of those were sensory words. Have them sort the sensory words by sight, touch, smell, sound, or taste. Students can keep a dictionary of sensory words in their Reading and Writing Portfolios and add to their list as they continue reading.

Formative Assessment

If the student...	Consider practicing these prerequisite skills:
had trouble thinking of sensory words	sort color, sounds, movement, taste, and texture words
had trouble identifying sensory or descriptive words	use word walls to highlight the five senses

Sense It Activity Cards

beach ball	sand	ocean	grass
cake	lemon	bird	dog
ice	tree	volcano	drum
boot	sun	marshmallow	blanket
toast	smoke	monkey bars	basketball
bell	telephone	sugar	bee
dirt	cloud	fire truck	stoplight

 ©2016 Hillary Wolfe, MA from *Writing Strategies for the Common Core*. This page may be reproduced for classroom use only.

Sense It Activity Spinner

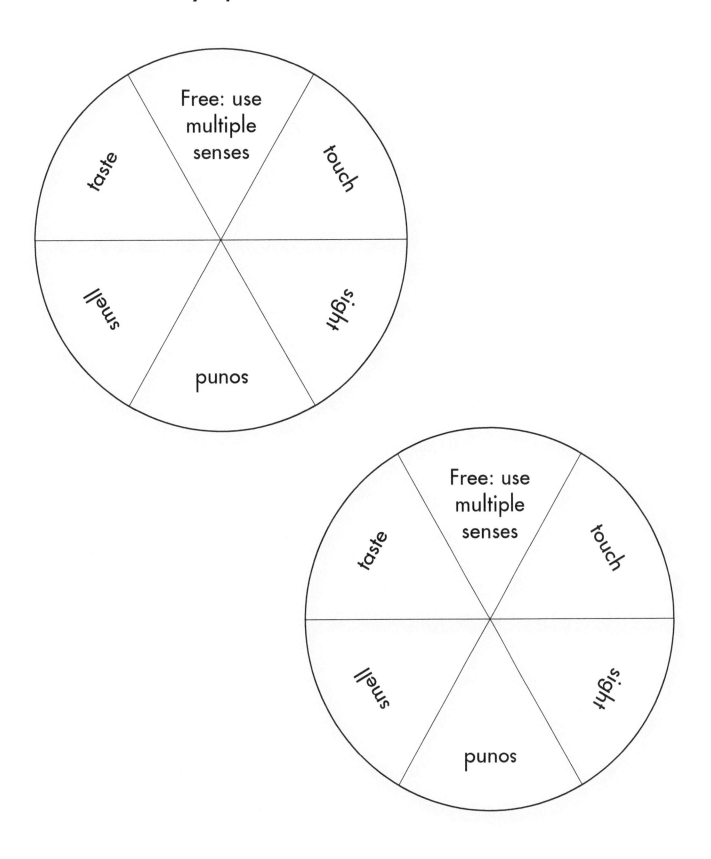

©2016 Hillary Wolfe, MA from *Writing Strategies for the Common Core*. This page may be reproduced for classroom use only.

Prewriting Mini-lesson: Processes

Materials

- Building blocks or 3-D shapes (one set per group of 3–4 students)
- Reading and Writing Portfolio
- *3-D Shapes* reference sheets, page 80
- *Build It! Cards* (one set per group of 3–4 students), page 81
- *Process Steps* activity sheet, page 82
- *Text Types and Purposes Chart*, page 26

Overview

Students will use explicit and precise terminology to describe three-dimensional objects; students will use the correct terminology to describe a sequential process.

Planning

Gather sets of building blocks that include as many different shapes as possible. If building blocks are not available, use found objects such as tissue boxes, bouncy balls, or other household items that represent different shapes.

Procedure

Modeling

1. Distribute copies of the *3-D Shapes* reference sheets to students, and give student groups access to one set of 3-D objects: a cube, a sphere, a cylinder, a pyramid, and a cone.

2. Hold up a cube and think aloud how to fill in the boxes on the reference sheet: "How many sides does this object have? Are the edges curved or straight? How many edges?" Have students use the actual objects to investigate as they answer the questions.

3. Have students fill in the sheets as you model, or have them work with partners to complete the sheet.

4. Tell students that when writing descriptively, the more precise they can be in their terminology, the clearer their descriptions will be. Model how to fill in the last column of the reference sheet by comparing the object to something: "The cube reminds me of a one-story building; the sphere looks like a handball."

Guided Practice

5. Ask students to work in groups of three or four. Distribute one set of the *Build It! Cards* to each group and one *Process Steps* activity sheet to each student.

6. Give each group of students a set of building blocks that include a variety of shapes. Have them work together for three to five minutes to build a structure using one of each shape. Extra shapes should be put to the side to be used in the game.

7. To play the game, have each student take turns pulling a *Build It! Card* and follow the directions on the card. If the move causes the structure to collapse, that student is out of the game (but can get back in with a "BACK IN THE GAME" card).

8. Have students play the game for several rounds. As they play, circulate and question the students about the characteristics of the shapes that made the move difficult or easy. Give students opportunities to practice using the vocabulary from their reference sheets.

Independent Practice

9. Ask students to answer the questions on the *Process Steps* activity sheet. Tell students they may use the blocks to help them determine the answers and the *3-D Shapes* reference sheets to cite the correct terminology.

10. Have students draw a picture or a diagram of their strongest structure. Challenge teams to recreate another group's structure.

Reading Connection

As students are reading, have them highlight or underline terms that describe a process, such as "First," "Next," "Last," or even "Be sure not to..." Have them circle those terms and add them to their "Process Words" pocket in their Reading and Writing Portfolios.

Formative Assessment

If the student...	Consider practicing these prerequisite skills:
had trouble thinking of precise terminology	content-specific vocabulary
had trouble sequencing	sorting pictures and labeling them with process or sequence words from a word bank

3-D Shapes

Name: _____

Directions: Fill in the columns below. In the last column, use clear and precise descriptions to state what the shape reminds you of as a comparison. An example has been done for you.

Shape	# of Sides	# of Edges		Comparison
		Curved	Straight	
cylinder	3	2	0	This shape reminds me of a canister
_____				
_____				
_____				
_____				

©2016 Hillary Wolfe, MA from *Writing Strategies for the Common Core*. This page may be reproduced for classroom use only.

Build It! Cards

Replace an object with a curved edge with an object with at least two straight edges.	Replace an object with a straight edge with an object with a curved edge.	Add an object with a curved edge to the top of the structure.	Remove one shape with a flat bottom.
Remove two shapes with flat sides.	Add one shape with a curved edge and a flat side to the structure.	BACK IN THE GAME!	Remove one shape.
Add one new shape.	Remove a shape with a straight edge and replace it with a shape with more than two sides.	Remove one shape.	BACK IN THE GAME!
Switch one shape from the bottom with one from the top.	Switch one shape from the bottom with one from the top.	BACK IN THE GAME!	Remove one shape.

©2016 Hillary Wolfe, MA from *Writing Strategies for the Common Core*. This page may be reproduced for classroom use only.

Processes

Name: _____

Process Steps

Directions: Reflect on the game you just played to answer the questions below. Use the *3-D Shapes* reference sheet to help you.

Which shape was the sturdiest? Why?

Which shape was the least sturdy? Why?

Describe step by step how you would build a structure using all five of the shapes. Explain each step and the placement of each shape along the way. Draw your sculpture on a separate sheet of paper.

First, I would start with _____

because _____

_____

_____

_____

_____

_____

_____

_____

_____

©2016 Hillary Wolfe, MA from *Writing Strategies for the Common Core*. This page may be reproduced for classroom use only.

Strategy Overview: Transitions

One key to strong writing is the organization. Starting a paragraph with a strong opening sentence, and finishing it with a closing thought compartmentalizes each idea and makes it accessible to the reader. The reader has time to process and understand each specific main idea before moving on to the next idea. Writing this way keeps the reader—and the writer—on track and helps minimize tangents that can lead them both astray.

Just as a paragraph deserves a strong structure with a clear beginning and ending, the entire body of the text also needs a strong structure, with a clear opening and a solid ending. An opening paragraph should get the reader interested and hold his or her attention. When the writer considers his or her audience and recognizes the purpose of the writing, it will be easier to set the tone of the piece from the beginning. Is the audience a peer, a group of adults, or the general public? Is it appropriate to start with a statistic, or would a personal anecdote be more attention grabbing? There are a number of choices the writer can make, each effective for different reasons. When a student understands some of the options for starting a piece of writing, according to the purpose of the task and the audience being addressed, the writing becomes clearer, stronger, and more meaningful.

From the reader's perspective, following the writer's thought process should be enjoyable and straightforward. The reader should have a clear sense of the direction that the writing is taking, and to that end, should clearly know when the journey is over. That is why a strong conclusion is so important. Have you ever absentmindedly eaten a bag of potato chips or chocolate chip cookies, maybe while watching television? You've been reaching in the bag over and over, and all of a sudden the bag is empty. How do you feel? Chances are, you feel frustrated that you didn't know you were almost out because had you known, you would have consciously savored that last chip or that final cookie.

The reader who is enjoying a piece of text wants to know that the end is coming so that he or she can savor every word and experience a satisfying sense of closure.

The following lessons can be used during the drafting stage of the writing process, when the student has organized his or her thoughts and is ready to end the text with a strong opening and a substantial closing.

Drafting Mini-lesson: Openings

Materials

- Reading and Writing Portfolio
- Paragraphs from the Main Ideas and Details Mini-lesson, pages 37–39
- *Explanatory Openings* activity sheet, page 86
- *Text Types and Purposes Chart,* page 26

Overview

Students will learn different options for creating strong opening paragraphs.

Planning

Display a picture of Earth from far away using a program such as Google Earth, Yahoo Maps, or Bing Maps. Choose a location that students would recognize, but zoom out to a distance where the location is not yet recognizable as a way to introduce the impact of starting with a general or broad idea versus a specific one. Students should have access to the paragraphs they wrote for the Main Ideas and Details activity.

Procedure

Modeling

1. Have students refer to their *Text Types and Purposes Chart.* Review the purpose of explanatory writing (*to explain*), argument (*to persuade*), and narrative (*to tell a story or relate a series of events*).
2. Show students how to zoom in to the Earth until a location is recognizable. Some students may have used the zoom feature on their cameras. Ask them what the advantage is of seeing a big picture versus a close-up. (The big picture gives a broader perspective, but a close-up lets you look at details you might miss.)
3. Write a list of generic versus specific sports terms on the board, such as *ball vs. football or tennis ball, score vs. touchdown or home run.* Explain to students that we can only explain so much using broad, generic examples and that specific details help us get a clearer idea of the author's meaning.
4. Tell students that writers need to give the audience a sense of the big picture so that the reader has a context within which to understand the specific example. The opening paragraph of any paper provides that big picture by outlining the main points that will be addressed. That way, the reader knows what to expect and looks forward to what he or she will find.
5. Tell students if the purpose of a text is to explain something, appeal to the reader by offering a good reason for knowing this information. Tell students they will learn two different ways to open a paper. The first is with a question, and the second is with a factual statement.
6. Write the word "Labrador" on the board. Tell students to pretend that this is their topic. What is the bigger picture? (dogs, pets)
7. Think aloud as you craft a question that centers on dogs or pets (e.g., *Which dog makes the best pet?* Or *Have you ever wished for a pet?*).
8. Tell students these questions are the "hook" for the text, and they provide a context for their topic: Labradors. Their next sentence should introduce the topic: *Labradors have a great reputation, which is why they make terrific pets.*

9. After the hook and the topic have been introduced, students should lay out the road map for their readers by listing the main ideas about their topic that will be addressed. In our example, the writer might say, *Labradors are protective, playful, and loyal.* This format (hook, topic, main ideas) will set up the writing.

10. Another option instead of a question is to start with a factual statement. (Note: The fact doesn't have to be accurate for this sample. Later, students can use real facts that they find through research.) Substitute a fact for the question in the example above: *Every year, Labradors are voted a favorite dog at dog shows. Labradors have a great reputation, which is why they make terrific pets.*

Guided Practice

11. Distribute copies of the *Explanatory Openings* activity sheet to each student.

12. Have students use the topics that they wrote about from the Main Ideas and Details Mini-lesson. Students will use this topic to fill out the "Question or Factual Statement" and "Topic" portions of their *Explanatory Openings* activity sheet.

13. Assist students as necessary as they think of their own questions and facts.

Independent Practice

14. Challenge students to add three main ideas to their *Explanatory Openings* activity sheet, based on the details they added to their original paragraphs.

15. Have students save these activity sheets in their Reading and Writing Portfolios as models of how to write opening paragraphs for explanatory writing.

Reading Connection

As students are reading, have them identify the characteristics of opening paragraphs that "hook" them into the text. Have them keep examples of strong openings in an "Openings" pocket in their Reading and Writing Portfolios.

Formative Assessment

If the student...	Consider practicing these prerequisite skills:
had trouble thinking of a question	using the 5 Ws
had trouble thinking of main ideas	create statements and then turn them into questions, significant details, such as definitions, descriptions, or comparisons

Explanatory Openings

Name: _____

Question or Factual Statement:
Topic:
Main Idea:
Main Idea:
Main Idea:

©2016 Hillary Wolfe, MA from *Writing Strategies for the Common Core*. This page may be reproduced for classroom use only.

Drafting Mini-lesson: Closings

Materials

- Reading and Writing Portfolio
- Paragraphs from the Main Ideas and Details Mini-lesson, pages 37–39
- *Explanatory Openings* activity sheet from previous lesson
- *Explanatory Closings* activity sheet, pages 89–91
- *Text Types and Purposes Chart,* page 26

Overview

Students will create parallel structures by using a similar technique in their closing paragraph as they used in their opening.

Planning

Create a version of the *Explanatory Openings* and *Explanatory Closings* activity sheets that can be used for display on an interactive whiteboard or with a document camera or overhead projector.

Procedure

Modeling

1. Have students refer to their *Explanatory Openings* activity sheets. Display the *Explanatory Openings* and *Explanatory Closings* side by side for students. The *Explanatory Openings* should still be filled out from the previous lesson.

2. Tell students they may have heard writing compared to a hamburger. This comparison simply shows that the opening and closing should consist of the same things and that the meat of the essay is in the middle. The opening and closing are different from the middle, but they are necessary to support everything that's asked for in the heart of the paper.

3. Point to the fact used in the opening line of the first paragraph. Tell students that if a fact is offered to start, then another fact should be offered in the closing. This fact should offer information that supports the fact used in the opening. For example, if the opening paragraph began with, "Every year, Labradors are voted a favorite dog at dog shows," then the closing paragraph could begin with, "The Labrador is America's number one breed." Model for students how to expand upon the fact used in the opening. If students used a question to start their opening paragraph, then the closing paragraph should begin by answering or responding to the question. The purpose of this is to bring the reader full circle and to encapsulate all the ideas in a cohesive structure. For example, if the opening paragraph began with, "What is so great about Labradors?," then the closing paragraph could begin with, "Lots of people wish for dogs that are loyal and playful. A Labrador would be a perfect pet." Model for students how to respond to the opening question with an answer.

4. Ask students to work with a partner to complete Part I of the *Explanatory Closings* activity sheet.

5. Show students how to restate their topic. Ask students to complete Part II of the *Explanatory Closings* sheet as you model.

6. Then show students how to pull a supporting detail from their paragraph and use it in place of restating the main idea. This will serve as a reminder or memento to the reader of the text. Ask students to complete Part III of the *Explanatory Closings* activity sheet as you model.

7. Finally, model how to write a "Now you know…" statement as the final concluding line. This should be a line that expresses what they have learned, what they now understand, or what they want the reader to understand. Have students complete Part IV of the *Explanatory Closings* activity sheet.

Guided Practice

8. Ask students to share their answers with a partner and to justify their choices. Circulate to be sure students are choosing appropriate facts and responses, transitions to the topic, and main ideas and details.

9. Have students work with partners and use the template on the activity sheet to create a closing paragraph that responds to the opening paragraph they created in the last session. Ask students to share their drafts, and have them explain their thinking. Post diverse examples so students recognize there are multiple ways to draft a successful closing paragraph.

Independent Practice

10. Instruct students to use the drafts of their openings and their *Explanatory Closings* activity sheet to write a sample closing paragraph.

Reading Connection

As students are reading, have them identify the characteristics of closing paragraphs that finalize what they read. Have them keep examples of strong closings in a "Closings" pocket in their Reading and Writing Portfolios.

Formative Assessment

If the student...	Consider practicing these prerequisite skills:
had trouble answering the question	stating facts in simple sentences
had trouble substantiating a fact	synonyms, adding adjectives or more nouns for description

Closings

Name: _____

Explanatory Closings

Part I
Read the facts below.

1. If this line were your opening sentence, "A sloth sleeps while hanging upside down!," which fact would you choose for the first sentence of your closing paragraph? (Try to choose a fact that would support and restate the opening.)

   a. I sleep under covers on a cozy bed.

   b. Sleeping upside down may look uncomfortable, but sloths seem to like it.

   c. Lions don't sleep at night; they hunt.

2. If this question was the opening line of your first paragraph, "Can you imagine having your bed in a tree?," which response would you choose for the first sentence of your closing paragraph? (Try to choose a response that would answer the opening question.)

   a. My bed is in a cozy room.

   b. A tree may be an unlikely place to sleep, but for a sloth, it's just right.

   c. No one wants a bed in a tree.

Part II
Read the topic statement below, and choose the best match that restates the topic for the closing paragraph.

1. Sloths are unusual animals.

   a. Of all the strange animals in the world, sloths are some of the strangest.

   b. Snakes are nothing like sloths.

   c. Kangaroos are also unusual but not as strange as sloths.

Part III

Read the main idea below. Choose the detail that you think best supports this idea:

One reason sloths are strange is because they sleep for long periods of time, usually while hanging.

   a. Because of their sleeping habits, sloths are considered lazy.
   b. If you met a sloth, you might think it was scary.
   c. Sloths can live a long time.

Part IV

Choose the best ending for this closing sentence about sloths:

Now I know...

   a. never to wake a sloth, especially if it's in a tree!
   b. how sloths in the zoo feel.
   c. what to make for dinner.

©2016 Hillary Wolfe, MA from *Writing Strategies for the Common Core*. This page may be reproduced for classroom use only.

Explanatory Closings

Name: _____

A new fact or an answer to the question (from opening):
Restate topic from:
Restate detail from main idea:
Restate detail from main idea:
Restate detail from main idea:
Now I know. . .

©2016 Hillary Wolfe, MA from *Writing Strategies for the Common Core*. This page may be reproduced for classroom use only.

Strategy Overview: Choose the Right Word

Students often think that once they have completed their draft, their work is over. To a large extent, it is. The hardest part of the writing—turning raw ideas into an organized piece of text—is difficult. But the work is not over yet.

The revision process requires a bit of trust on the part of the writer. It is difficult to have your hard work critiqued and criticized. But students need to recognize that a little distance helps them improve on their work to make it even better and that it is not in any way an indication that they didn't do their draft correctly or that they forgot something. The purpose of communicating through writing is to get your point across. If your reader missed your point, then you must find another way, a better way, or a more effective way to make your point. Getting another opinion helps focus that feedback and provides concrete ways for students to make the small adjustments necessary.

Many students are used to an extracurricular activity, such as piano. When the teacher gives tips about how to improve, it is not a criticism of the player's talent. It is merely a helpful tip from an objective observer who knows just what to look for.

Help students feel comfortable with the revision process by including them in co-constructing the review criteria. Use the objectives of the Prewriting and Drafting Mini-lessons as your guide, and ask students what a "finished" paper should include. Use their suggestions and build a rubric that they all feel is attainable. Then, have students review each other's work, looking for very specific criteria outlined on the rubric. This is not a time for students to offer personal opinions. They either see evidence of the objectives or they don't. That will provide each student author with a concise guide as to what still needs to be done on the paper before it is ready for publishing.

Revising Mini-lesson: Words That Explain

Materials

- Pencil and sharpener (for demonstration)
- Chart paper
- Sticky notes
- *Describe Your Day* activity sheet, page 96
- *All Aboard Explanation Starters,* page 97
- *Making Tracks Cards* (one set for 4 students), page 98

Overview

Students will practice inserting sequence or process transition words into explanatory writing. They will discover how specific transition words support specific text structures and build a reference document to use later for the culminating project.

Planning

Prepare enough sets of the *Making Tracks Cards* and laminate if desired. Use a sheet of chart paper that can be posted and used for reference.

Procedure

Modeling

1. Hold up a pencil and a sharpener, and ask students to watch as you wordlessly insert the pencil and turn the crank (or push the button) and sharpen the pencil.

2. Ask students to think without speaking about all the things you did, in the order you did them. Have students pull out a sheet of paper if they need to and model sharpening the pencil again. This time, ask students to silently write down all the steps to sharpening a pencil as you are completing them. Have students turn to a partner and share their descriptions.

3. Ask a few students to read their descriptions aloud. On a sheet of chart paper, use sticky notes and post the transition words that the students use, such as *first, then, after that,* or *next.* Have several students come to the poster and, with help from the students in their seats, rearrange the sticky notes so that the transition words appear in a logical order (e.g., *first, next, then, finally*).

4. Tell students that explanatory writing usually uses a special kind of structure. In order to explain how to do something, the text is ordered as a process of steps or a sequence. Sometimes, explanatory texts explain why something happened, as in cause and effect. Ask students to brainstorm some cause-effect words and post their responses on the chart paper. (Draw a separate column if you like and label it "Cause-Effect." Label the first column "Process." Label a third column "Compare.") Share that one other kind of informational writing compares things.

5. Ask students to brainstorm comparison words and post those as well. Distribute the *Describe Your Day* activity sheets. Have students share with a partner an example of a process that they do every day (e.g., brush teeth, walk to school). Have them also share a cause-effect they experience (e.g., if they eat breakfast slowly, then they will be late for school). Finally, ask students to think of a comparison they could make with another student (e.g., one student may walk while another takes the bus.) After they share with their partners, have students fill in the first question on their activity sheets.

Guided Practice

6. Tell students they are going to play a game. Distribute the *Making Tracks Cards* (one set for four students) and the *All Aboard Explanation Starters* sheets (one per student). Explain the game: One student is the conductor. He or she will choose one of explanation starters from the sheet. The conductor reads the starting sentence aloud.

7. The next player will choose a *Making Tracks Card*. Depending on the instructions on the card, the player must write the next line of the explanation. For example, if the card makes a U-turn, the player must use one of the transition words listed on the card to tell the next line or step in the explanation. He or she then puts the card on the table, and the next player takes a turn, drawing a card and saying the next line. When the play returns to the conductor, he or she does not draw but must use a conclusion card to write the last line. Everyone returns his or her card to the deck and reshuffles. Then, the person to his or her right becomes the next conductor, and the game resumes.

Independent Practice

8. Have students display all the *Making Tracks Cards*. Ask if any group would like to share one of their co-constructed explanations. Ask students to describe how they made choices as they wrote their lines (e.g., a cause-effect explanation required different types of words than a process).

9. Ask students to use a new sheet of paper to write an explanation about something they do during the day. Have them return to their activity sheets, or tell them they may use some ideas from the *All Aboard Explanation Starters* sheet or a new idea altogether.

10. Stipulate that students' explanations must contain at least four unique transition words and the words should help the reader understand whether the explanation is a process, a cause-effect, or a comparison. Students may look at the *Making Tracks Cards* to help them.

11. Have students share their explanations with a partner or small group and see if the listeners can determine which type of explanation they heard. Have students give feedback about the words they heard (or didn't hear) and how the explanations could be improved.

Reading Connection

As students read, have them identify the transition words they find and write them on individual cards. Have them identify the structure of the text as well (process, cause-effect, comparison). Have students keep the cards in the "Transition Words" pockets in their Reading and Writing Portfolios.

Formative Assessment

If the student...	Consider practicing these prerequisite skills:
had trouble thinking of transition words	ordinals, numbering
had trouble thinking of comparison words	sorting activities to stress commonalities

Words That Explain

Name: _____

Describe Your Day

Directions: Think of your daily routines. Describe one process, one cause-effect, and one comparison you can make about your day in the boxes below.

A process I do is...	A cause-effect in my day is...	I can compare...to... because

Choose one of the examples above and write a longer explanation using some of the words below. Use these diagrams to help you sequence your explanation.

Process:

First → Then → Next → Finally

Cause-Effect:

If... → then... →

Compare:

Similar to → ← Because ← Different from Because →

©2016 Hillary Wolfe, MA from *Writing Strategies for the Common Core*. This page may be reproduced for classroom use only.

Words That Explain

All Aboard Explanation Starters

Directions: The conductor reads a starter sentence aloud. The player to the right chooses a *Making Tracks Card* and uses that card to start the next line of the explanation. (For example, if the card makes a U-turn, the player must use one of the transition words listed on the card to tell the next line or step in the explanation.) Put the card on the table, and the next player takes a turn, drawing a card and saying the next line. When play returns to the conductor, he or she does not draw but must use a conclusion card to write the last line. Everyone returns his or her card to the deck and reshuffles, and the next conductor begins the next round.

Starter 1:
Every Saturday morning my dad makes breakfast for the family.

Starter 2:
There are only a few things to remember about riding a bike.

Starter 3:
My cousin lives in a big city, but my best friend lives on a ranch.

Starter 4:
Want to know how to be successful in school?

©2016 Hillary Wolfe, MA from *Writing Strategies for the Common Core*. This page may be reproduced for classroom use only.

Making Tracks Cards

Conclusion Card Finally…	**Conclusion Card** At last…	**Conclusion Card** Therefore…
Conclusion Card So that's why…	**Advance the Tale** ✚ And then… Next… Additionally…	**Advance the Tale** ✚ Second… Third… Later…
Advance the Tale ↱ But then… However… Unexpectedly…	**Advance the Tale** ↱ Don't forget… It's hard to believe, but… Unfortunately…	**Advance the Tale** ↩ On the other hand… Nevertheless… Actually…
Show Cause-Effect � → First…then… If…then… When…then…	**Show Cause-Effect** ▶→ As a result of…then… Imagine…then… …caused…which then…	**Show Cause-Effect** ↔ Because…then… Once…then… Since…then…
Show a Comparison ◯ Is similar to… Reminds me of… Is just like…	**Show a Comparison** ◯ Is more than… Is less than… Is better/worse than…	**Show a Comparison** 🚫 Is different from… Does not seem like… Is not the same as…

©2016 Hillary Wolfe, MA from *Writing Strategies for the Common Core*. This page may be reproduced for classroom use only.

Revising Mini-lesson: Sentence Structure

Materials
- Chart paper
- Die or spinner
- Timers
- *Sentence Structures* activity sheet, page 102
- *Simple Sentence Cards* (one set for each group of 4 students), page 103
- *Bigger and Better, Shorter and Simpler* game board (one for each group of 4 students), pages 104–105

Overview
Students will work with partners and race to create a variety of sentence structures by playing a game that directs them to transform simple sentences into complex sentences, or vice versa.

Preparation
Be sure that students have been introduced to different sentence structures, including simple sentences, compound sentences, and complex sentences. Students should have a working knowledge of nouns, verbs, adjectives, adverbs, prepositional phrases, and conjunctions. Copy the *Simple Sentence Cards* and cut them apart. Make several copies of the game board and laminate the cards and game boards for durability.

Procedure
Modeling

1. Tell students that the way to revise is to create varied and interesting sentences. Good writing has a variety of sentence structures, which keeps the reader interested.

2. Distribute the *Sentence Structures* activity sheets to students. Draw a three-column chart on a sheet of chart paper. Label the first column "Simple." In this column, write the simple sentence *The dog barks*. Ask students to identify the parts of this sentence (noun, verb). Label, highlight, or underline the noun and verb in the sentence. Have students copy this onto their activity sheets. Remind students that they can build more complicated sentences. Label the second column "Compound." In this column, write *The dog barks, and the cat meows*. Ask students how this sentence is different from the first. Chart their responses, and label the parts of the sentence, including the conjunction. Tell students a compound sentence could be broken into two stand-alone sentences.

3. Have students copy this onto their activity sheets.

4. Label the third column "Complex." Write the sentence *The dog barks whenever a squirrel enters the yard.* Have students share with a partner how this sentence is different from the first two. Identify the independent and dependent clauses, and label the parts of speech. Have students copy this onto their activity sheets. Have students write definitions of each type of sentence in their own words on their sheets.

5. Have students get into groups of four. Distribute the *Bigger and Better, Shorter and Simpler* game board, one timer, and the *Simple Sentence Cards* to groups. Explain the game: Each group has two teams who will take turns rolling a die and moving along a game board. When they land on a square, they draw a *Simple Sentence Card* and follow the direction on the space where they landed. Teams will have 30 seconds to confer and create a new sentence. If the sentence makes sense and meets the criteria, they will earn a point. If the sentence does not make sense, the team must stay on the space and on their next turn, draw a different *Simple Sentence Card* and try again. The die is then passed to the other team, who repeats the process. The first team to reach the finish line wins.

Independent Practice

6. Discuss the different types of sentences that students wrote. Ask teams to post their best examples of simple, compound, and complex sentences in the appropriate column on the chart, as well as on their activity sheets.

7. Have students pull out a piece of writing from their portfolios, or revisit the paragraphs they started in the earlier lessons of this chapter. Have them trade papers with a peer, and direct the peer to highlight or underline one example of a simple sentence, a compound sentence, and a complex sentence. If they cannot find an example, students can note which type of sentence was missing.

8. Have students return papers to their owners, and task students to change each underlined sentence: A simple sentence could be changed to a compound or complex sentence, a compound sentence could be changed into two simple sentences, and so on.

9. On the bottom of their activity sheets, ask students to fill in the reflection question.

10. After checking in the activity sheets, ask students to keep these sheets in their Reading and Writing Portfolios in the "References" pocket.

Reading Connection

As students read, have them identify different sentence structures and keep them as models. Assign students specific types of structures to look for when they read, such as independent clauses. If students can't find enough variety in their texts, have them choose three to five simple sentences and rewrite them in a more interesting way. Then encourage students to examine how the sentences were rewritten and identify the grammatical features that were changed or added to make the sentence more complex.

Formative Assessment

If the student...	Consider practicing these prerequisite skills:
did not understand one or more of the terms	direct instruction in verbs, nouns, and adjectives
did not change or add to the structure of the simple sentence	review simple, complex, and compound sentences; review conjunctions; punctuation

Sentence Structures

Name: _____

Directions: Write a sample sentence in each column. Label the parts of speech. In the box at the bottom of each column, write a definition of each type of sentence in your own words.

Simple Sentence	Compound Sentence	Complex Sentence
Example:	Example:	Example:
Definition:	Definition:	Definition:
My best simple sentence:	My best compound sentence:	My best complex sentence:

Reflection: On the lines below, explain how you changed one sentence.

One sentence I rewrote was:

_____

to _____

by _____

_____.

©2016 Hillary Wolfe, MA from *Writing Strategies for the Common Core*. This page may be reproduced for classroom use only.

Simple Sentence Cards

The dog barks.	The sun rises.	Breakfast is served.	Oranges grow on trees.
Kids ride bikes.	Doctors check for illness.	The dentist gives out toothbrushes.	Bears hibernate.
The moon glows.	Leaves fall.	Candles burn.	Rain clouds are forming.
Wear your ice skates.	The milk spilled.	A garden grows.	A bird flies.
The door slammed.	Cars speed.	A baby cries.	Brush her hair.

©2016 Hillary Wolfe, MA from *Writing Strategies for the Common Core*. This page may be reproduced for classroom use only.

Bigger and Better, Shorter and Simpler

Playing the game: Each group has two teams who will take turns rolling a die and moving along a game board. When they land on a square, they draw a *Simple Sentence Card* and follow the directions on the space where they landed. Teams will have 30 seconds to confer and create a new sentence. If the sentence makes sense and meets the criteria, they will earn a point. If the sentence does not make sense or the team cannot successfully create a sentence, they must stay on the space until their next turn, when they draw a different card and try again. The die is then passed to the other team. The first team to reach the finish line wins.

Start

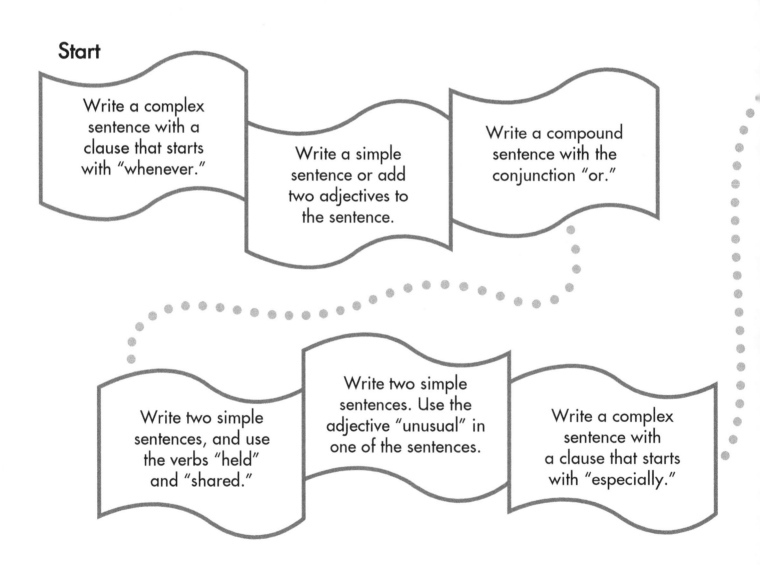

Write a complex sentence with a clause that starts with "whenever."

Write a simple sentence or add two adjectives to the sentence.

Write a compound sentence with the conjunction "or."

Write two simple sentences, and use the verbs "held" and "shared."

Write two simple sentences. Use the adjective "unusual" in one of the sentences.

Write a complex sentence with a clause that starts with "especially."

©2016 Hillary Wolfe, MA from *Writing Strategies for the Common Core*. This page may be reproduced for classroom use only.

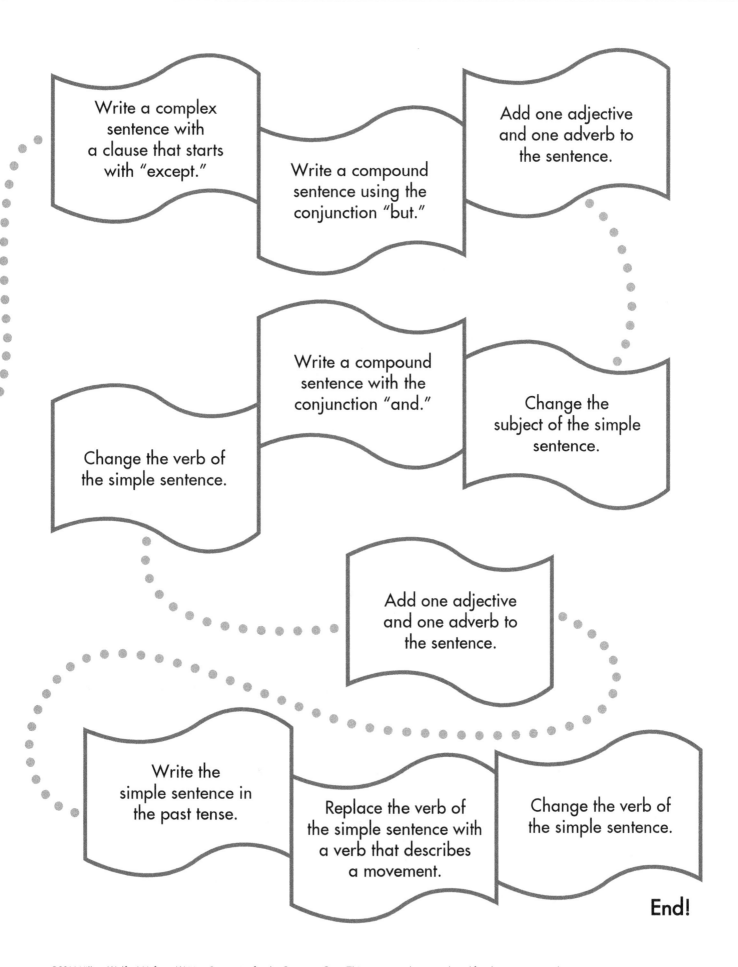

Write a complex sentence with a clause that starts with "except."

Write a compound sentence using the conjunction "but."

Add one adjective and one adverb to the sentence.

Write a compound sentence with the conjunction "and."

Change the subject of the simple sentence.

Change the verb of the simple sentence.

Add one adjective and one adverb to the sentence.

Write the simple sentence in the past tense.

Replace the verb of the simple sentence with a verb that describes a movement.

Change the verb of the simple sentence.

End!

©2016 Hillary Wolfe, MA from *Writing Strategies for the Common Core*. This page may be reproduced for classroom use only.

Culminating Project Ideas

Language Arts

Write a visitor's guide for your hometown, including step-by-step directions to local points of interest and descriptions of events that occur throughout the year.

Texts:

A City Through Time by Philip Steele (nonfiction), published by DK Children

Arctic Peoples by Robin S. Doak (nonfiction), published by Heinemann-Raintree

Big City Sights by Anita Yasuda (fiction), published by Stone Arch Books

New in Town, Raven's Pass by Steve Brezenoff (fiction), published by Stone Arch Books

The Kid's Guide to San Francisco by Eileen Ogintz (nonfiction), published by Globe Pequot Press

Social Studies

Write and perform a dialogue between two historical figures from different eras, comparing their lives, where they live, or their perspectives of an important event.

Texts:

César: ¡Sí, Se Puede!/Yes, We Can! (poetry) by Carmen T. Bernier-Grand, published by Two Lions

Leonardo da Vinci Gets a Do-Over by Mark P. Friedlander (nonfiction), published by Science, Naturally!

Sonia Sotomayor: A Judge Grows in the Bronx/La Juez Que Creció en el Bronx (nonfiction) by Jonah Winter, published by Atheneum Books for Young Readers

What Color Is My World? The Lost History of African-American Inventors by Kareem Abdul-Jabbar and Raymond Obstfeld (nonfiction), published by Candlewick

Mathematics

Use geoboards and describe the characteristics of a polygon, including the number of sides, angles, and how to find the perimeter.

Texts:

Buildings and Structures by Andrew Solway (nonfiction), published by Heinemann-Raintree

Cathedral: The Story of Its Construction by David Macaulay (nonfiction), published by HMH Books for Young Readers

Science

Explain why a glass with ice "sweats." Design an experiment to test your theory.

Texts:

In Search of the Fog Zombie: A Mystery about Matter (Summer Camp Science Mysteries) by Lynda Beauregard (fiction), published by Graphic Universe

Temperature by Casey Rand (nonfiction), by Heinemann-Raintree

The Dynamic World of Chemical Reactions with Max Axiom, Super Scientist by Agnieszka Biskup (nonfiction), published by Capstone

 ©2016 Hillary Wolfe, MA from *Writing Strategies for the Common Core*. This page may be reproduced for classroom use only.

Additional Resources

Essay Frames
Structure of a body paragraph:

    I. Topic sentence—tells main idea

        a. Describe

        b. State a fact

        c. Make a comparison

   II. Closing sentence—mirrors main idea

  III. Body paragraph #1—A. What is the first idea you want to talk about? _____

  IV. Write a **topic sentence** that addresses this idea. Start with an **ADJECTIVE**.

_____

        a. Use **sensory words** to describe this idea.

_____

_____

_____

_____

        b. State a **fact** about this idea.

_____

_____

_____

©2016 Hillary Wolfe, MA from *Writing Strategies for the Common Core*. This page may be reproduced for classroom use only.

c. Make a **comparison** between this idea and something similar to or different from it.

_____

_____

_____

V. Think of an **adjective** that is synonymous to the adjective you used above. Write a **closing sentence** using that adjective.

_____

_____

HOMEWORK: USE THIS WORKSHEET TO WRITE YOUR BODY PARAGRAPH.

©2016 Hillary Wolfe, MA from *Writing Strategies for the Common Core*. This page may be reproduced for classroom use only.

Rubrics: Point-based

Directions: Assign points for any or all of the following elements, or focus on one or two elements or paragraphs at a time, and have students revise their work to earn additional points.

Format — _____ points

    Three paragraphs (introduction,
        one body paragraph, conclusion)   _____

    Typed or handwritten in ink   _____

    Proper indentation   _____

    Spelling/punctuation   _____

Writing Process/Materials — _____ points

    Observation journals   _____

    Body paragraph worksheet   _____

    Body paragraph rough draft   _____

    Opening/closing paragraph worksheet   _____

    Opening/closing paragraph rough draft   _____

    Peer edit/self-edit   _____

Opening Paragraph — _____ points

    One interesting fact   _____

    Topic   _____

    Thesis   _____

    Main ideas   _____

Body Paragraph — _____ points

    Topic sentence starts with an adjective   _____

    Topic sentence addresses first main idea   _____

    Describe using sensory descriptions   _____

    State a fact about the main idea   _____

    Explain a cause/effect   _____

    Use transition words   _____

    Closing sentence   _____

    Closing sentence uses synonymous adjective   _____

Closing Paragraph — _____ points

    Another interesting fact   _____

    Restate topic in different words   _____

    Thesis restates your stance about the topic   _____

    Main Ideas   _____

    Clincher — one line about what you've learned   _____

    Title (matches clincher)   _____

©2016 Hillary Wolfe, MA from *Writing Strategies for the Common Core*. This page may be reproduced for classroom use only.

Analytic Rubric

	Above Average (4)	Sufficient (3)	Developing (2)	Needs Improvement (1)
Introduces topic clearly and group-related information				
Develops the topic with relevant facts, definitions, concrete details, quotations, or other information and examples				
Uses appropriate transitions to create cohesion and clarify the relationships among ideas and concepts				
Uses precise language and domain-specific vocabulary to inform about or explain the topic				
Provides a concluding statement or section that follows from and supports the information or explanation presented				
Demonstrates correct grammar and spelling				
Produces clear and coherent writing in which the development, organization, and style are appropriate to task, purpose, and audience				
Develops and strengthens writing as needed by planning, revising, editing, rewriting, or trying a new approach, focusing on how well purpose and audience have been addressed				
Uses technology, including the Internet, to produce and publish writing and link to and cite sources				
Draws evidence from literary or informational texts to support analysis, reflection, and research				

©2016 Hillary Wolfe, MA from *Writing Strategies for the Common Core*. This page may be reproduced for classroom use only.

Holistic Rubric

4	The student writes informative/explanatory texts to examine a topic and convey ideas, concepts, and information through the selection, organization, and analysis of relevant content. The focus of the work is clearly identified and is supported by clear and relevant details. The organizational structure is strong and cohesive and informs the content. Mechanical or grammatical errors are minimal.
3	The focus of the work is fairly clear and is supported by somewhat relevant details. Information is presented in a fairly logical and coherent manner. Minimal errors do not detract from overall meaning and understanding.
2	The focus of the work is not easily identified, and supporting ideas are not fully connected; or only minimal and superficial amounts of evidence are presented as support. The organization is present, but not thoughtful nor cohesive. There are several noticeable misspellings and mechanical errors.
1	The focus is unclear and a central idea is lacking. There is little related evidence to support the thesis, and information is presented in a disorganized or stream-of-consciousness manner. Misspellings and mechanical errors are frequent and detract from the ability to comprehend the work.

(Adapted from *Assessment: Types of Rubrics, DePaul University*)

©2016 Hillary Wolfe, MA from *Writing Strategies for the Common Core*. This page may be reproduced for classroom use only.

Chapter 4

Argument Text

Overview of the Genre

Purpose

An argument is a way to state a claim and back it up with evidence, usually to persuade or convince others. The student has to decide the best way to back up his or her claims, and choose evidence that will be appropriate and reliable. There are two key pieces of information that a student must consider when writing an argument: the topic or reason for writing and the audience.

The topic or reason for writing gives students a basis for the text structure. If the reason for writing is to present a solution to a problem, the student may choose a problem-solution structure. If the reason for writing is to present the benefit of one position over another, the structure may be claim/counterclaim. Students may be writing in a number of formats, including a letter, an editorial, or a report, or they may be crafting a commercial, staging a debate, or creating a campaign poster.

Before writing an argument piece, the author must understand the characteristics of each of these text structures and formats so he or she can make an informed decision about which approach will be best suited to the topic.

Audience

The author must then also consider the audience for the piece. Understanding the likely recipients will determine the tone of the piece as well as the word choice. If the topic has to do with making a change in the community or school, the audience will probably be adults. Therefore, the tone should be serious and the word choice more fact based. If the topic has to do with solving a problem, the audience may be younger peers, so the tone may be humorous, and the word choice may lean toward the colloquial or even slang.

Having a strong grasp of the components of argument text will help students make better choices when they write and help them critically analyze persuasive writing when they read it. Argument text has many of the same characteristics as explanatory text: a strong organizational structure, main ideas and supporting details, and an evocative conclusion. What distinguishes argument text from explanatory or informational text, though, is the types of details that are used to support the claims and that it can call the audience to action.

Reading Strategy: Inferring

An inference is made when the reader combines clues in the text with his or her own personal experiences. Expressing an opinion means stating a point of view. Being persuasive means using facts to support that opinion and showing why the opinion is credible. Facts can include statements from authoritative sources, visual evidence, statistics and data, or personal experience. Students must be critical thinkers and readers who can make inferences based on the facts they encounter and their own experiences. These tools will help them determine the reliability of what they read.

Focus: Reliable Facts

By making inferences about the data they encounter, students will start to recognize how important it is to have the whole story. Data that is incomplete is like a picture that only shows a scene from one perspective. How reliable is a fact if only one view is represented? It is important for students to consider the information that is *not* available as much as the information that *is* available. In a 21st century world where access to information is immediate, students need to cultivate their inference skills so they can validate the accuracy and credibility of the information they read.

Reading Strategy: Questioning

As a reader, students need to ask questions of the text. They should be starting to question what they read and form healthy doubts about the reliability of the information they encounter. Students are typically taught to ask the "W" questions—who, what, where, when, why, and how—when they prepare to write about a topic. As a reader, there are different "W" questions they should ask, such as:

- *Who was the author?*
- *Does the author have specific credentials or authority on this topic?*
- *What was the purpose of writing this piece? Did the author have a hidden agenda?*
- *Where did this information come from? How reliable is the source?*
- *When was this written (recently or long ago)?*
- *Why did the author take this perspective? Was the author biased in any way?*
- *How did the author get this information? How is this information relevant to the topic?*

Being an informed consumer of information is just as important as being a responsible producer of information.

Focus: Personal Connections

A personal connection will tie a reader to a point of view because that point of view will be more relatable. Being able to put oneself in another person's shoes is the basis of empathy, and the more we feel like we relate to someone, the more likely we are to agree with him or her.

When they read, students should pay attention to the personal connections the author is trying to make. Does the author include short anecdotes? Does the author describe his or her family, background, home life, hometown, or neighbors? These examples help the reader connect to the author's point of view.

Students should also pay attention to pictures and illustrations, which can portray strong emotions without any words. Imagine seeing a picture of a baby laughing or a puppy caught in a cage. Each of these images will evoke powerful feelings that will sway our opinions.

Prerequisite Skills

Because this unit will focus on the reading strategies of asking questions and inferring, students will need practice with these tools. Provide Mini-lessons that model how to question a text by thinking aloud using the consumer questions referenced on the previous page. Have students look at pictures (visual texts) and ask them to make inferences based on what they see, including the colors, the fonts, and how images and texts are placed upon the page.

Academic Vocabulary

In argument especially, words will have subtle shades of meaning. Give students exposure to different contexts for common academic terms to help them be comfortable seeing the shades of meaning and ambiguity of certain words. Such ambiguity will matter when every word counts.

Use sentence frames to help students incorporate academic terms into their responses, both verbal and written, and insist on complete sentences when students answer aloud. Incorporating academic terms into everyday conversation will raise the level of academic discourse within the classroom.

Sample Planning Calendar

Monday	Tuesday	Wednesday	Thursday	Friday
RI: Text structures—problem-solution	RP: Text structures—finding problem-solution structures	RI: Text structures—claim-counterclaim	RP: Text structures—finding claim-counterclaim structures	WI/WP: Write an opinion paragraph using one of the structures
RI: Questioning—finding facts	RP: Questioning—using consumer questions	WI: Writing facts vs. writing opinions	WP: Back up opinions with facts	WI/WP: Facts vs. personal experiences V: Qualitative transitions (contrasts and additions)
RI: Making connections to other texts	RP: Making connections—find connections in other texts	RI: Text structures—how to organize ideas in an argument	WI/WP: Text structures—how to organize ideas in an argument	WI/WP: Using graphic organizers for prewriting
WI/WP: Revising, using figurative language to add power	G: Revising, looking for fragments and compound/complex sentences	WP: Editing TEST PREP	TEST PREP	TEST PREP

Legend

RI = Reading Instruction
RP = Reading Practice
WI = Writing Instruction
WP = Writing Practice
V   = Vocabulary
G   = Grammar

Strategy Overview: Have an Opinion!

Students may seem to have opinions about everything, or they may be unsure how they feel about anything. As they grow, they will learn how to use facts and information to help them form opinions and gain the confidence to defend those opinions. Students need practice using evidence to back up their claims, so they get in the habit of relying on research or personal experiences as the basis of their opinions.

Persuasion and argument are not used as verbs in this section. This type of writing is not intended to teach students how to be combative. The goal of studying and writing opinion text is to show students the importance of evidence. In this case, argument is used as a noun, representing a point of view or a stance. The more evidence a student can find to support a stance, the more convincing the argument and the more credible the writing.

In this section, students will practice choosing facts to support their opinions that they have determined are credible and reliable. They will also see how personal examples can provide relevant evidence as well, by connecting the reader to the writer's experience. They will learn to recognize the use of facts and personal examples in text they read and also in visual texts, including pictures, diagrams, and graphs. Through guided prewriting activities, students will practice supporting their own opinions in different ways. As they begin to write drafts, they will see how their understanding of audience, purpose, and tone can and should influence the structure of their argument, as well as their word choices. Finally, they will see how to revise their work with relevant transition words and interesting sentence structures.

Consider giving students a culminating project that requires them to apply all their new skills in an integrated way. By studying and practicing the art of argument, students will gain confidence in critical thinking.

Prewriting Mini-lesson: Facts and Opinions

Materials

- Chart paper
- Timer
- Reading and Writing Portfolio
- *Facts in Four Recording Sheet* (one for each group of 3–4 students), page 119
- *Opinion Statement Cards* (one set for each group of 3–4 students), page 120
- *Text Types and Purposes Chart,* page 26

Overview

Students will brainstorm and collect facts to support opinions.

Planning

Prepare enough cards for each group of students. Laminate the *Facts in Four Recording Sheets* so students can reuse them with dry-erase markers.

Procedures

Modeling

1. Introduce the word *opinion.* Tell students that an opinion is something we believe is true, but others may disagree and have a different point of view. Each person's point of view is his or her opinion. Draw a two-column chart on a sheet of chart paper. Label one column "Opinions." Have students brainstorm some examples of opinions about their classroom, the school, or their neighborhood. Chart their ideas.

2. Introduce the word *fact.* Tell students that a fact is something we can prove or that everyone agrees is true. Have students brainstorm some examples of facts about their classroom, the school, or their neighborhood. Chart their ideas in the second column on the chart and label the column "Facts."

3. Explain to students that a way to support an opinion is by backing it up with facts. For example, saying that chocolate is the best ice cream is an opinion; if you find data that shows that more people like chocolate than any other flavor, you have backed up your opinion with a fact that supports it.

4. Choose one of the opinions listed on the *Opinion Statement Cards,* and tell students you are going to show them how to play a game. Use an overhead projector and display a copy of the *Facts in Four Recording Sheet.* Explain to students that they will work in groups of four and that they are to list the first initial of each of their first names down the side.

5. Set the timer for three minutes. Have students race against you to come up with as many facts as they can about the opinion, using the initials as the first letter of the facts they choose. Show them the sample on their recording sheets.

Guided Practice

6. Distribute the *Opinion Statement Cards*. Have students work in groups of four and take turns choosing an opinion card and then racing to complete the recording sheets.

7. Continue playing until all students have had an opportunity to choose an opinion card.

8. Have students work in pairs and choose one opinion to write about. Ask students to select the facts that are the most relevant and credible.

Independent Practice

9. Have students use the organizer to choose their facts. Then ask students to work independently to write a paragraph about an opinion from the opinion cards.

10. Tell students to choose facts from the game, but encourage them to also think of other facts or to research more information that could support their opinions.

11. Have students share their paragraphs with a peer and get feedback about the facts they chose.

Reading Connection

Tell students that facts are usually easy to find, because often they include data, statistics, or a graph. Ask students to examine texts for examples of facts, and have them underline or highlight the clue word or visual that helped them know they had found a fact. Have students keep track of these examples by listing them in their Reading and Writing Portfolios.

Formative Assessment

If the student...	Consider practicing these prerequisite skills:
had trouble identifying facts	clue words, such as "studies show" or "research proves"
had trouble matching facts to the initials	synonyms and multiple meanings of words

Facts and Opinions

Name: _____

Facts in Four Recording Sheet

Directions: List the first initial of each player's name down the side of the recording sheet. Take turns choosing an opinion card, set the timer for three minutes, and race to complete the sheets, listing one fact for each initial. See the example row that has been completed for you. Continue playing until all players have had an opportunity to choose an opinion card.

		Opinion statement: Limit television to 30 minutes a day.
Support with a fact that starts with the letter:	**Example: W**	Watching television for too long can hurt your eyes.
	First initial of player 1:	
	First initial of player 2:	
	First initial of player 3:	
	First initial of player 4:	

©2016 Hillary Wolfe, MA from *Writing Strategies for the Common Core*. This page may be reproduced for classroom use only.

Opinion Statement Cards

Chocolate ice cream is the best.	Dogs are the best pets.	Animals should not be kept in a zoo.
Kids should not have more than 20 minutes of homework a night.	Cell phones at school are OK.	School uniforms are a good idea.
Video games are bad for you.	Junk food should be allowed at school.	Kids only need six hours of sleep a night.
Everyone should get Fridays off.	Bounce houses are dangerous.	Too many cartoons are bad for kids.
Chocolate milk should be allowed at school.	Limit television to 30 minutes a day.	Kids should get paid for doing chores.
Everyone needs to take care of the environment.	There should be fines for wasting water.	Girls and boys should learn all the same sports.

©2016 Hillary Wolfe, MA from *Writing Strategies for the Common Core*. This page may be reproduced for classroom use only.

Prewriting Mini-lesson: Supporting Details

Materials

- Chart paper
- *Support Strategies* activity sheets (one for each pair of students), pages 123–124
- *Opinion Statement Cards* (from the previous lesson; one set for each pair of students)

Overview

Students will learn to identify different types of details they can use to support their opinions, including credible sources, data and statistics, or personal experiences.

Planning

Use the cards from the previous lesson, or have students create their own opinion cards to include. Laminate the *Support Strategies* activity sheets so students can reuse them.

Procedure

Modeling

1. Remind students that when writing argument text, the author wants to find strong ways to support his or her opinions and ideas. In the last lesson, they learned that facts can support an opinion. But there are other ways to support their ideas too.

2. Write an opinion on the board, such as *Dogs make the best pets.* Ask students if they think this is true or not. Draw a four-column chart on the board or on chart paper. Label the first column "Fact."

3. Choose one or two students to offer a fact that supports or disproves this opinion. For example, *Dogs are loyal and live a long time*, would support that opinion, but *Dogs are messy and need a lot of exercise* would be a good fact against the opinion. Write their suggestions in the "Fact" column.

4. Tell students you need to find another way to support this opinion. Write "Expert" at the top of the second column on the chart. Ask, "Is there an expert I could ask about dogs who might give me more information?" Let students suggest experts, such as veterinarians, pet store owners, or zookeepers. List their suggestions in the second column.

5. Label the third column "Data and Statistics." Ask students what kind of research they could do to prove their opinion? Guide students to suggest looking for data about how many people have dogs as pets or statistics about how dogs improve the lives of their owners. Ask students to brainstorm where they could find that information. List their responses in the third column of the chart.

6. Label the last column "Personal Example." Ask students to share some personal examples about dogs, either from their own families or from friends. Have students paraphrase their stories in the fourth column of the chart.

Guided Practice

7. Have students work with partners. Distribute one set of *Opinion Statement Cards* and one *Support Strategies* activity sheet to each pair of students.

8. Have partners take turns choosing a card and then filling in the categories on the worksheet together.

9. Post four sheets of chart paper around the room. Write one opinion at the top of each sheet of chart paper. Once all partners have completed their worksheets, have them rotate around the room and write their best support for that opinion on the chart paper. If their idea was already used by another pair of students, they must choose something different to add.

10. Once everyone has had a chance to add a supporting detail to the charts, have students do a gallery walk to read all the different ways their classmates were able to support their opinions.

Independent Practice

11. Have students choose one opinion statement and write a brief paragraph arguing for or against the statement. Tell students they don't need to do actual research, but have them include one fact, one expert statement, one piece of data, and one personal example to support their opinion.

12. For follow-up, ask students to do the actual research and write a credible paragraph about the opinion statement. Have them color code the research they do so that a fact is written in orange, a quote from an expert is written in green, data or statistics are written in blue, and a personal example is written in purple.

Reading Connection

As students read argument text, have them use the same color-coding technique to identify the type of details the author uses to support his or her opinions. Ask students how they were able to determine which type of detail the author was using. Were there clue words? Have students discuss the types of evidence that are most effective to support an opinion. Guide them to recognize that different types of support are effective for different reasons—it all depends on the purpose of the piece and the audience to whom it is directed. See if students can start to create some "rules" about argument writing. Post their ideas around the room for reference and to use later on.

Formative Assessment

If the student...	Consider practicing these prerequisite skills:
had trouble identifying experts	Have students brainstorm the type of jobs associated with each topic and link the professions with the people who study or work at those jobs.
had trouble identifying type of data	Review the purposes of surveys, statistics, graphs, and timelines, and practice how to read them; review headings, captions, and data labels.

Supporting Details

Name: _____

Support Strategies

Directions: Work with a partner. Choose one opinion card and write the statement. Fill in answers for each column: "Fact," "Expert," "Data/Statistic," "Personal Example."

Opinion statement:			
Fact *Write one fact that supports or disproves this opinion.*	**Expert** *Who could you ask for more information? What might he/she be able to tell you?*	**Data/Statistics** *What kind of research could you do to help you find more information? What would you want to know?*	**Personal Example** *Do you have any experience with this topic? Does someone you know have any experience?*

©2016 Hillary Wolfe, MA from *Writing Strategies for the Common Core*. This page may be reproduced for classroom use only.

Opinion statement:

Fact Write one fact that supports or disproves this opinion.	Expert Who could you ask for more information? What might he/she be able to tell you?	Data/Statistics What kind of research could you do to help you find more information? What would you want to know?	Personal Example Do you have any experience with this topic? Does someone you know have any experience?

Opinion statement:

Fact Write one fact that supports or disproves this opinion.	Expert Who could you ask for more information? What might he/she be able to tell you?	Data/Statistics What kind of research could you do to help you find more information? What would you want to know?	Personal Example Do you have any experience with this topic? Does someone you know have any experience?

 ©2016 Hillary Wolfe, MA from *Writing Strategies for the Common Core*. This page may be reproduced for classroom use only.

Strategy Overview: Audience, Tone, and Purpose

Never underestimate the importance of knowing your audience. Nothing can derail a presentation faster than failing to understand the intended recipients and their expectations. Consider paying for a ticket to a movie called *The Nightmare*. Most likely, you're expecting to see a horror film. The title of the movie creates an image in your mind, a presupposition, that you are about to see a scary movie. However, the movie is really a documentary about clinical psychologists who document children's dreams. This is a very different movie! Chances are, the typical movie-goer would be very disappointed and unlikely to sit through this whole movie.

Once students know their audience, this will help them make decisions about the tone you will take (respectful, funny, formal, casual) and the words they will use (colloquial, academic, jargon, emotion laden). The first Mini-lesson will show students how to use their understanding of audience to choose a tone and make strong word decisions.

Understanding audience is only one piece of the puzzle. Students also must have a clear sense of the purpose of their writing. What are they trying to achieve? What is the outcome they're hoping to accomplish as a result of this writing? If a writer wants to offer a solution, he will first need to present and explain the problem and then offer one or more solutions with a clear explanation about why these will be effective. If a writer is explaining why one view is better than another, she must state her point of view and then acknowledge the other perspective. Then she can offer a counterpoint by introducing better or more credible evidence.

Understanding the purpose helps writers make another choice about their writing. It helps them decide on the structure. How will students best present their information? If solving a problem, using specific transition words will help the audience understand that a variety of good solutions are being presented. If presenting a claim and acknowledging a counterclaim, students might choose different transition words and set up their argument in a different way as well. Recognizing the purpose helps writers take the most appropriate approach.

Drafting Mini-lesson: Thematic Writing

Materials

- Chart paper
- Document camera
- *Themed Party Activity Sheet,* page 128

Overview

Students will plan a themed party and brainstorm terms that support the theme.

Planning

Choose a piece of text to model themes that has visual as well as textual details that all work together cohesively. A picture book might be a good start for students who are struggling with this idea. Consider using this activity to launch a culminating project. After students brainstorm ideas for their themed party, have them build a Pinterest board or scrapbook page to represent the party.

Procedure

Modeling

1. Introduce the word *thematic.* Ask students what they think it means, and have them give some examples. Write their ideas on a sheet of chart paper and display it.

2. Explain to students that we see evidence of themes all around us. For example, ask students what kinds of things they would expect to see at a rodeo. Write "rodeo" on a sheet of chart paper, and list students' ideas, such as horses, Western hats and boots, cowboys, clowns, and so on. Have students pair-share some other examples of places or events that center around a theme.

3. Ask students how the details help support the theme. Add some of their comments to the chart paper. Guide students to discuss how visual elements, sounds, smells, music, and so on all contribute to the theme of a place.

4. Introduce the word *cohesive,* and explain that in writing, it means that the author tries to choose details that work well together in order to better support a theme.

5. Display a text on the document camera and point out how the author used text features as well as language to support a specific idea. For example, a scientific text will most likely contain diagrams, charts, and step-by-step procedures. But a fantasy book will probably contain drawings of invented settings and use made-up names for locations. Explain that these features of text help us understand what kind of text we are reading, just as much as the words chosen by the author.

Guided Practice

6. Have students work with partners or in small groups. Distribute copies of the *Themed Party Activity Sheets* to each student.

7. Instruct students to choose a theme for an imaginary party. Have them write their theme choice on their activity sheets.

8. Next, ask students to work together to think of all the specific elements that need to be included for a successful party: decorations, food, music, location, costumes, etc.

9. Tell students to describe each of the elements on their activity sheets.

10. Ask students to use the template on their activity sheets to draft an invitation to their party. Have them describe some of the specific elements to their invited guests that will persuade them to attend.

11. Challenge students to design an invitation on the computer that contains specific elements: a unique font, a picture, and a border. Ask them to justify the font they choose, the picture and border, and any word choices they made. How did the occasion help them choose their theme? Did the guest list influence their word choices?

Reading Connection

Ask students to watch a cartoon on television or an animated feature movie. Animators make use of thematic elements, such as colors, music, background images, voices, or drawing style, to support the theme of the show. Have students identify three thematic elements that support the piece and explain why these elements add to the overall experience.

Formative Assessment

If the student...	Consider practicing these prerequisite skills:
had trouble thinking of enough terminology	start with a more universal theme
had trouble coming up with a theme	list amusement parks or themed restaurants and describe the specific characteristics of each

Thematic Writing

Name: _____

Themed Party Activity Sheet

Directions: Imagine you are throwing a party, and you are to choose a specific theme. Write the occasion and your theme on the lines below. Next, create an imaginary guest list. Then imagine the decorations, food, music, and location for your party. Fill in these items below. On a separate sheet of paper or on the computer, design and write an invitation to your party and persuade guests to attend by describing all the elements of the party you have planned.

Occasion:

_____

Theme:

_____

Guests:

_____

_____

Decorations:

_____

Food:

_____

Music:

_____

Location:

_____

 ©2016 Hillary Wolfe, MA from *Writing Strategies for the Common Core*. This page may be reproduced for classroom use only.

Drafting Mini-lesson: Structuring an Argument

Materials

- Chart paper
- Reading and Writing Portfolio
- *Community Affair* activity sheet, page 131
- *Drafting a Newspaper Ad Checklist,* page 132

Overview

Students will practice using the cause-and-effect text structure to convince an audience to attend a special event. Students will learn to acknowledge and address a counterargument.

Planning

Have students research neighborhood community events or study local newspapers to discover upcoming activities in your area. If there are not enough options, have students brainstorm an event or activity they would like to see in their town, such as a fair or a farmers' market.

Procedure

Modeling

1. Ask students if they have ever attended a local carnival, fair, or community event. What did they enjoy about that experience? How did they learn about it? What made them interested in attending?

2. Tell students that understanding the outcome of an action, or the effect, can convince us to take that action. For example, students may be afraid to get a flu shot, but when they understand that the shot can keep them from getting sick, it can be easier to persuade them to get the shot. This is called understanding cause and effect.

4. On a sheet of chart paper, write the students' definitions of cause and effect. Tell students that causes usually are described in writing with words like *if, when, try to, because.* Write these ideas on the chart paper, and add other ideas that students may have.

5. Tell students that effects usually are described in writing with words like *then, resulting in, therefore, causes, creates.* Write these ideas on the chart paper, and add other ideas that students may have.

6. Distribute copies of the *Community Affair* activity sheets to students. Draw two boxes on the board, with an arrow between them. Have students refer to their *Community Affair* activity sheets. Explain how the first box shows an event: going to a pumpkin patch. Ask students to help you identify some of the reasons people would want to go to a pumpkin patch. Write their ideas in the second box: get pumpkins, go to a petting zoo, have a fun day outside.

7. Notice above the first box is the word "If." Above the second box is the word "Then." Tell students "*If* you come to a pumpkin patch, then you will get to choose as many pumpkins as you can carry."

8. Tell students not everyone wants to go to the pumpkin patch. Notice the third box says, "But." Ask students what would be an obstacle or a reason not to go to the pumpkin patch (carrying lots of pumpkins can be difficult, etc.). Write their ideas in the third box.

9. Notice the fourth box says "So." What would be a way to overcome the obstacle (bring a wagon, etc.)?

Guided Practice

10. Tell students to work with a partner and, in the remaining boxes, write the name of an event from the brainstormed list they created earlier or think of some other community events they would like to advertise. Together, come up with at least two reasons why people should attend this event.
11. Then, have students work together to think of one obstacle or reason people might not want to attend the event. Write that reason in the third box.
12. Finally, have students describe a way to overcome the obstacle, and write it in the fourth box.
13. Have students share their ideas and do a gallery walk, so all students can comment on the work of their classmates.

Independent Practice

14. Ask students to choose one event they would like to write an ad about and to draft a description of the event, including two reasons to attend.
15. Be sure students include an obstacle they think people might have and address how to overcome that obstacle.
16. Have students use the *Drafting a Newspaper Ad Checklist* to self-evaluate their drafts, or use the checklist for peer editing.

Reading Connection

As students are reading persuasive or argument texts, have them identify the cause-and-effect words by highlighting or underlining them. Have them search for counterarguments and see how the author addressed the counterargument. If the author did not address a counterargument, how could they add a counterargument to the text?

Formative Assessment

If the student...	Consider practicing these prerequisite skills:
had trouble identifying cause and effect	review sequences and processes
had trouble thinking of counterarguments	review conflicts and obstacles

Structuring an Argument

Name: _____

Community Affair

Directions: Write about a community event in the "If" box. Fill in the "Then" box with the effects of attending the event. In the next box, "But," list an obstacle that might need to be overcome. Offer a solution to it in the "So" box. An example has been done for you.

If...

Then...

You come to the pumpkin patch,	You will get to choose as many pumpkins as you can carry, **And...** You can play at the petting zoo,

But...

So...

You might think you are too small to carry a lot of pumpkins,	You can bring a wagon instead!

Now you try it!

If...

Then...

	And...

But...

So...

©2016 Hillary Wolfe, MA from *Writing Strategies for the Common Core*. This page may be reproduced for classroom use only.

Structuring an Argument

Name: _____

Drafting a Newspaper Ad Checklist

_____ I named an event or activity that takes place in my community with an invitation to attend.

_____ I described the event or activity.

_____ I gave two examples of what might happen if guests attend ("If…, then…").

_____ I acknowledged one counterargument ("But…").

_____ I offered a way to overcome the obstacle suggested by the counterargument ("So…").

_____ I thanked my readers for their time and used a closing statement.

 ©2016 Hillary Wolfe, MA from *Writing Strategies for the Common Core*. This page may be reproduced for classroom use only.

Strategy Overview: Transitions Support the Structure

There is a tendency among young writers to overuse simple sentence structures. This is understandable, as students may not have had a lot of practice with more complex or compound sentences. The more opportunities they have to experiment with sentence structures, the more interesting their writing will become.

Crafting complex sentences is not an innate skill. Therefore, students need authentic reasons to add sentence variety. In argument writing, transitions play a key structural role in the writing and offer a great opportunity to practice using different sentence structures.

Part of the revising process, then, should ask students to look closely at their writing and see where they can insert transitions, and by so doing, add some sentence variety. Introduce different types of transitions and keep posters with transitions visible around the room. Encourage students to document interesting sentence structures that they find in their reading and to use those examples as models for their own writing.

In addition, students should start practicing recognizing the transitions that are used within specific text structures. For example, a process or explanatory text will probably use transitions that represent a sequence. But a text with a problem-solution structure will probably use transitions such as "if," "but," "so," or "therefore." Have students start to sort their transitions into categories, and see if they can justify the structure of the text based on the kinds of transitions that are used.

Revising Mini-lesson: Transitions

Materials

- Chart paper
- Reading and Writing Portfolio
- A short piece of argument text
- *Transition Words Sorting Cards* (one set for each pair or group of 3 students), pages 136–137
- *Text Types and Purposes Chart*, page 26

Overview

Students will practice using different transition words to support an argument or opinion.

Planning

Make enough copies of the cards to distribute to pairs or groups of three students. Laminate the cards before cutting them to make them sturdier.

Have students use their *Text Types and Purposes Charts* to help them, and have them create a pocket in their Reading and Writing Portfolios for collecting examples of different transition words and interesting sentences.

Procedure

Modeling

1. Refer students to the previous lesson, and remind them that they were able to structure a counter-argument by acknowledging and addressing any conflict or obstacle to the argument they made. Remind them that they used the words "if," "then," "but," and "so."

2. Tell students that those words represent *transitions.* Co-construct a definition for *transition word*, and write the definition on the chart paper. Some responses might include: a word that links two ideas, a word or phrase that introduces an opposite idea, or a word that tells what is coming next.

3. Ask students to brainstorm a list of transition words, such as "for example," "next," and "consequently."

4. Have students work with a partner or in groups of three. Give each group a set of *Transition Words Sorting Cards*. Ask students to skim through the cards and choose any words they would like to add to the charted list on the board.

Guided Practice

5. Ask students to work together to sort their cards into three categories and to label each category. There is no "right" way to do this. Students may sort and label the categories any way they wish, but let them know they will be expected to justify their selections and the labels they give to each category. Tell students they may use their *Text Types and Purposes Charts* to help them.

6. Ask a few students to share their lists and the labels they gave to their categories. Discuss any words they had trouble fitting into a category. What did other groups do with that word?

7. Distribute copies of a short piece of argument text, or display a text and read it aloud. After reading the text, ask students if they would like to re-sort any words, add any words, or change the labels on their categories. Give students time to modify their word sorts, and have a few students share out.

8. Ask students what they noticed about the transition words in the text they read. How were they used? Were they at the beginnings of sentences, at the ends of sentences, or in the middle?

Independent Practice

9. Have students look at another piece of argument text, and have them work with a partner to underline or highlight the transition words they found.

10. Ask students to write an explanation of how the transition words were used in the text and to justify their explanations with evidence from the text.

11. Have students revise a piece of their own writing. Tell them to add or change three sentences that use transitions, and challenge them to use one transition at the beginning of a sentence, one in the middle of a sentence, and one at the end of a sentence.

Reading Connection

As students read persuasive text, have them continue to highlight the transition words they find and to use those words to explain and justify their ideas about the structure of the text. Have them compare and contrast texts based on the transition words and text structures. When they are ready to write, encourage students to plan ahead the text structure they would like to use. Then, select transition words that align with that structure.

Formative Assessment

If the student...	Consider practicing these prerequisite skills:
had trouble categorizing the transition words	provide a pre-established set of labels for the categories
had trouble using transition words at the beginning, middle, or end of a sentence	provide sentence frames with the transition words already inserted and allow practice writing around them

Transition Words Sorting Cards

Additionally	Furthermore	Likewise	Of course
However	Plus	On the other hand	But
Too	Consequently	Just like	Then
Also	Not to mention	Again	By the same token
Equally important	First	Next	Finally
In addition	As a matter of fact	In the same way as	Different from
Although	Even though	Besides	Rather

 ©2016 Hillary Wolfe, MA from *Writing Strategies for the Common Core*. This page may be reproduced for classroom use only.

Instead	While	Yet	Otherwise
With this in mind	So that	Since	Even if
In case	In order to	Unless	For one thing
For example	For instance	In fact	Especially
Specifically	And another point	As a result	Therefore
Because	In the long run	Usually	Mostly
As shown	Generally speaking	To sum up	So

©2016 Hillary Wolfe, MA from *Writing Strategies for the Common Core*. This page may be reproduced for classroom use only.

Revising Mini-lesson: Linking Ideas

Materials

- Scratch paper
- Document camera
- *Transition Words Sorting Cards* (from the previous lesson, one set for each group of 4 students)
- *Claim Trains* activity sheets (copies per group of 4 students), pages 140–141
- *Text Types and Purposes Chart,* page 26

Overview

Students will play a game similar to dominoes to practice building credible arguments using unique transition words.

Planning

Use the *Transition Words Sorting Cards* from the previous lesson, and have students work in groups of four. Laminate the *Claim Trains* activity sheets, and provide students with scratch paper to record their sentences.

Procedure

Modeling

1. Tell students they will be playing a game that will help them build sentences using a variety of transition words. These kinds of sentences represent examples of how to support an opinion with an example, a fact, or a counterclaim.

2. Use a document camera to display the *Claim Trains* activity sheet and several *Transition Words Sorting Cards.* In the center of the *Claim Trains* sheet, write a simple opinion. (Dogs are the best pets.)

3. Draw one *Transition Words Sorting Card,* such as "for example." Model how to mark one of the tracks and support the opinion with a sentence that uses the phrase on the card.

4. Tell students they will all continue to add to a sentence until they run out of ideas. The person who can mark up an entire track wins the point. Once a card has been played, it is removed from the deck.

   The next player then writes a new opinion in the center, and begins a new track. The game continues until all the cards are gone or all the tracks have been used.

Guided Practice

5. Have students play in groups of four. Distribute the *Claim Trains* sheets and one set of cards to each group. Give students scratch paper to write down the sentences if they need to in order to remember them. Assign one student in each group to be the recorder.

6. Assign a topic to students and have them write an argument either for or against it. Instruct students to use transition words in their supporting sentences.

7. Have students share their writing with a peer, and instruct them to circle or highlight all the transition words they can find. If a transition word is repeated, encourage the students to replace it with a unique word. Have them refer to their *Text Types and Purposes Charts* for help.

Reading Connection

Have students use the *Claim Trains* sheet while they read to note the transition words used in text. Did they notice any repeats? Would they have used different words? Why or why not?

Formative Assessment

If the student...	Consider practicing these prerequisite skills:
had trouble using transition words	offer simpler versions of the words, or add an example to the backs of the cards to model for students how the word can be used

Linking Ideas

Claim Trains

Directions: Player 1 writes a simple opinion in the center circle. (e.g., Dogs are the best pets.) That player also draws one *Transition Words Sorting Card,* such as "for example." All players support the opinion with a sentence that uses the phrase on the card. Players add a mark in the chain for every sentence they can create. Players continue to add to a sentence until they run out of ideas. The person who places the final mark on the train wins the point for that track. Once a card has been played, the player removes it from the deck.

Player 2 creates a new opinion for the center and begins a new track. The game continues until all the cards are gone or all the tracks have been used.

 ©2016 Hillary Wolfe, MA from *Writing Strategies for the Common Core*. This page may be reproduced for classroom use only.

Claim Trains

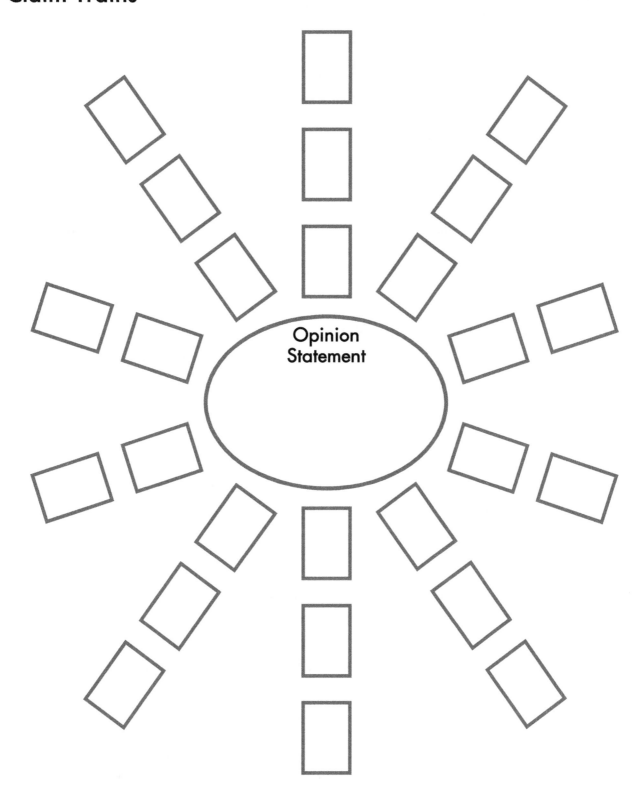

Opinion Statement

©2016 Hillary Wolfe, MA from *Writing Strategies for the Common Core*. This page may be reproduced for classroom use only.

Culminating Project Ideas

Language Arts

Write a visitor's guide for a new student about how to make the most of all the school has to offer. Describe the special events and the fun things that happen in your school. Use facts and personal experiences in your explanation.

Texts:

CITIES: Discover How They Work with 25 Projects (Build It Yourself) by Kathleen M. Reilly and Tom Casteel (nonfiction), published by Nomad Press

I Am Malala: How One Girl Stood Up for Education and Changed the World (Young Readers Edition) by Malala Yousafzai and Patricia McCormick (nonfiction), published by Little, Brown Books for Young Readers

When You Reach Me by Rebecca Stead (fiction), published by Yearling Newbery

Social Studies

Collaborate with a group to write rules for the playground. How would you enforce these rules? How will you get other students to agree to follow these rules?

Texts:

Beach Volleyball Is No Joke by Anita Yasuda (fiction), published by Capstone

Founding Mothers: Remembering the Ladies by Cokie Roberts and Diane Goode (nonfiction), published by HarperCollins

How Can We Help Out in Our Community? by Tony Stead (nonfiction), published by Capstone

We the People: The Story of Our Constitution by Lynne Cheney and Greg Harlin (nonfiction), published by W. W. Norton & Company

Mathematics

Advocate for planting a garden in a specific place on the playground, around the school, or in containers. Include the kinds of plants you want to grow, and research the amount of space, soil, water, and light the plants will need. Use that data to support your opinions about where to create your garden.

Texts:

Sodbury Season (Volume 1) by David Miadovnik (fiction), published by CreateSpace Independent Publishing Platform

Sustaining our Natural Resources by Jen Green (nonfiction), published by Heinemann-Raintree

The Good Garden: How One Family Went from Hunger to Having Enough (Citizenkid), by Katie Smith Milway and Sylvie Daigneault (nonfiction), published by Kids Can Press

 ©2016 Hillary Wolfe, MA from *Writing Strategies for the Common Core*. This page may be reproduced for classroom use only.

Science

Write a letter to NASA convincing them why you should be the first elementary school student in space. Use facts and personal examples to make your point, and address any counterarguments that NASA might have.

Texts:

13 Planets: The Latest View of the Solar System by David A. Aguilar (nonfiction), published by National Geographic for Kids

Beyond the Solar System: Exploring Galaxies, Black Holes, Alien Planets, and More by Mary Kay Carson (nonfiction), published by Chicago Review Press

Buzz Beaker and the Outer Space Trip by Cari Meister (fiction), published by Capstone

Time for Kids Book of How: All About Space by the editors of *TIME for Kids* magazine, published by TIME for Kids

©2016 Hillary Wolfe, MA from *Writing Strategies for the Common Core*. This page may be reproduced for classroom use only.

Additional Resources

Argument Frames

Plan Your Opening Paragraph

Who is your **audience**?

_____

What is your **tone**?

_____

What is the **purpose** for writing this argument?

_____

Start Your Essay Rough Draft Here

Start with a **question** as your hook:

_____

State the **topic:** _____

_____

Thesis: State your opinion about this topic.

_____

Main Ideas:

List the facts and examples you plan to use to support your opinion.

_____

_____

_____

_____

_____

©2016 Hillary Wolfe, MA from *Writing Strategies for the Common Core*. This page may be reproduced for classroom use only.

Body Paragraph Frame

I. State the fact or example in your topic sentence.
    Start this sentence with an adverb.

    _____

    a. Support your fact or example with further explanation, such as data,
        research, or a personal story.

        _____

        _____

        _____

    b. Address a counterargument. Use a transition word in this sentence.

        _____

        _____

        _____

    c. Closing sentence: Use another **adverb**, and restate your topic sentence.

        _____

        _____

        _____

HOMEWORK: USE THIS WORKSHEET TO WRITE YOUR BODY PARAGRAPHS—
DUE TOMORROW!

©2016 Hillary Wolfe, MA from *Writing Strategies for the Common Core*. This page may be reproduced for classroom use only.

Closing Paragraph Frame

Answer the hook question from your opening:

_____

Restate the topic substituting different words:

_____

Restate the thesis:

_____

Restate details from the main ideas:

_____

Clincher: End with a friendly plea for your case:

_____

_____

_____

_____

_____

Use this as your title: _____

 ©2016 Hillary Wolfe, MA from *Writing Strategies for the Common Core*. This page may be reproduced for classroom use only.

Rubrics: Point-based

Directions: Assign points for any or all of the following elements, or focus on one or two elements or paragraphs at a time, and have students revise their work to earn additional points.

Format — _____ **points**

Three paragraphs (introduction, one body paragraph, conclusion)	_____
Typed or handwritten in ink	_____
Proper indentation	_____
Spelling/punctuation	_____

Writing Process/Materials — _____ **points**

Transition worksheet	_____
Body paragraph worksheet	_____
Body paragraph rough draft	_____
Opening/closing paragraph worksheet	_____
Opening/closing paragraph rough draft	_____
Peer edit/self-edit	_____

Opening Paragraph — _____ **points**

One question	_____
Topic	_____
Thesis	_____
Main ideas	_____

Body Paragraph — _____ **points**

Topic sentence starts with an adverb	_____
Topic sentence addresses first main idea	_____
Use a fact or personal example	_____
Support the fact or example with explanation	_____
Use transition words	_____
Closing sentence with adverb	_____

Closing Paragraph — _____ **points**

Answer the opening question	_____
Restate topic in different words	_____
Thesis restates your opinion about the topic	_____
Main idea	_____
Clincher	_____
Title (matches clincher)	_____

©2016 Hillary Wolfe, MA from *Writing Strategies for the Common Core*. This page may be reproduced for classroom use only.

Analytic Rubric

	Above Average (4)	Sufficient (3)	Developing (2)	Needs Improvement (1)
Introduces claim(s), acknowledges alternate or opposing claims, and organizes the reasons and evidence logically				
Supports claim(s) with logical reasoning and relevant evidence, using accurate, credible sources and demonstrating an understanding of the topic or text				
Uses words, phrases, and clauses to create cohesion and clarify the relationships among claim(s), reasons, and evidence				
Establishes and maintains a formal style				
Provides a concluding statement or section that follows from and supports the argument presented				
Produces clear and coherent writing in which the development, organization, and style are appropriate to task, purpose, and audience				
Develops and strengthens writing as needed by planning, revising, editing, rewriting, or trying a new approach, focusing on how well purpose and audience have been addressed				
Uses technology, including the Internet, to produce and publish writing and link to and cite sources				

©2016 Hillary Wolfe, MA from *Writing Strategies for the Common Core*. This page may be reproduced for classroom use only.

	Above Average (4)	Sufficient (3)	Developing (2)	Needs Improvement (1)
Draws evidence from literary or informational texts to support analysis, reflection, and research				
Traces and evaluates the argument and specific claims in a text, assessing whether the reasoning is sound and the evidence is relevant and sufficient to support the claims				

©2016 Hillary Wolfe, MA from *Writing Strategies for the Common Core*. This page may be reproduced for classroom use only.

Holistic Rubric

4	The student writes arguments to support claims with clear reasons and relevant evidence. The claim set forth is clearly identified and is supported by clear and relevant details, including logical and emotional appeals as appropriate to audience and tone. The organizational structure is strong and cohesive and informs the content. Mechanical or grammatical errors are minimal.
3	The claim is fairly clear and is supported by somewhat relevant details, including reasons and evidence. Information is presented in a fairly logical and coherent manner. Minimal errors do not detract from overall meaning and understanding.
2	The claim is not clearly identified, and supporting evidence is not fully connected; or only minimal and superficial amounts of evidence are presented as support. The organization is present but is not thoughtful or cohesive. There are several noticeable misspellings and mechanical errors.
1	The claim is unclear and a central idea is lacking. There is little related evidence to support the claim, and information is presented in a disorganized manner. Misspellings and mechanical errors are frequent and detract from the ability to comprehend the work.

(Adapted from *Assessment: Types of Rubrics, DePaul University*)

©2016 Hillary Wolfe, MA from *Writing Strategies for the Common Core*. This page may be reproduced for classroom use only.

Chapter 5

Narrative Text

Overview of the Genre

Purpose

Narrative text relates a series of events, either real or invented. Most associated with storytelling, narrative can be a biography, a fictional account, or the relation of an historical incident.

Why do we tell stories? Stories help us learn about the world, the past, and other cultures, and ultimately, they help us understand ourselves. Seeing the universality of peoples' feelings, fears, hopes, and dreams connects us to others and shows us that we are not alone in the world. Common experiences unite people across time and space and help us understand one another with empathy and compassion.

A narrative is often viewed as the most natural form of writing for students since it allows them to tell a story. Many teachers start the school year by asking students to write a personal narrative as a way to get to know them. Students are natural storytellers, and narrative writing comes easily to them. In this book, narrative is introduced last because it allows for a looser structure. Once students have successfully mastered the structured formats of explanatory or argument writing, they will be more accustomed to writing to criteria and may be more receptive to having structural choices as they write their narratives. Explanatory and argument writing allows students to practice identifying and using predictable text structures, and narrative writing gives students some freedom to experiment. Giving students lots of practice with specific structures first prepares them with choices and options for writing narratives later on.

Reading Strategy: Summarizing

Focus: Context

The goal of reading a narrative is to understand some universal truth. But to do this, a reader must have background information.

Start by examining the story in the context of the setting and point of view. The setting will provide information about the location, the time period, the time of year, and the events going on around the story. The setting offers a frame to support the story and will help students make inferences about the theme of the story.

Next, recognize who is telling the story. The point of view of the narrator or main character is important, as it is the lens through which the reader experiences the events. Point of view can be very subjective, and students should start to realize that one event can be interpreted in many different ways, depending on the point of view. Help students recognize the point of view and also analyze why the author chose that point of view. Was it to gain sympathy from the reader? Was it a way to put the reader in an uncomfortable position, to help him or her examine his or her own beliefs?

Focus: Conflict

A narrative can be characterized first by its structure. Whether the events are sequential, told in flashback, or some combination of these, there should be a logical progression from one event to the next. Typically, a narrative structure will have some common components.

The narrative will begin with an introduction of the setting, the characters, and most importantly, the conflict. The conflict is the element that elevates a narrative from a series of unrelated events to a thematic journey in which the character must either overcome an obstacle, face a fear, or fulfill a quest. Once the conflict is established, the events drive the story to a climax (when the conflict is finally addressed) and a resolution (when the outcome is realized). The story concludes with the realization that something has changed for the character and that his or her life will forever be altered by the experiences recounted in the narrative.

Conflicts can be broadly characterized as man vs. man, man vs. self, or man vs. nature. But there are other kinds of conflicts, such as overcoming an obstacle or a physical handicap or trying to reach a goal. Students need to use sequencing strategies to keep track of the events as they occur and decide how the events build to a climax and, finally, to the resolution.

Reading Strategy: Making Connections

Focus: Personal Examples

We ask students to make connections when they read in order to activate prior knowledge and to help them get invested in the text. Authors help readers do this by providing relatable experiences. When the reader can see him- or herself through the eyes of a character, the reader experiences empathy and can imagine experiencing the events of the story as if they were happening to him or her. This doesn't mean that the story has to be realistic. On the contrary, students often are completely transfixed by a fantasy character living in a completely fictional environment. But that just speaks to the power of relating to the character through similar emotions and personality traits.

Point out places where students might feel especially connected to a character as they read, and ask them to put themselves in the character's shoes. Encourage these connections so students start to see the value of including personal reflections in their own writing. The more they can reveal their own thoughts and feelings, the more their readers will be able to relate to them as well.

Focus: Word Choice

Characters reveal a lot about their personalities by the words and language choices they make. Accents, slang, and speaking styles help the reader picture and understand the character. Just as important as physical attributes, how a character communicates reveals his or her personality and can help readers make predictions about how the character might behave in different situations.

Through dialogue, we get to know the characters and decide whether we like them. Their likability makes them relatable, and when we can relate to a character, we can put ourselves in his or her shoes and see things from a new perspective. Seeing things through the eyes of a character is one of the most effective ways to promote a theme.

Prerequisite Skills

Because this unit will focus on the reading strategies of summarizing, using text structures, and making connections, students will need practice with these tools. Provide Mini-lessons on character traits and descriptive writing. Provide students with graphic organizers that will help them map out narratives as they read, so they can find a clear beginning, middle, and end. Have them create visuals that not only portray the settings but touch on thematic elements, such as darkness to portray sadness or fear.

Specific Content-area Vocabulary

Provide specific definitions for character traits, beyond simplistic descriptions like *happy, sad, angry,* or *funny.* Point out that most characters can't be boiled down to one characteristic. In fact, it is the combination of traits that make them interesting and relatable.

Finally, as students begin to practice making inferences, assist them in making deeper connections to their own personal experiences. Text analysis is difficult and not an innate skill. Students need practice justifying their thinking, using evidence from the text as well as inferential information they connected from their own backgrounds. This is where many students will need to start integrating several reading strategies at once, to visualize, ask questions, connect, predict, and infer so they can finally summarize and generalize a bigger and deeper understanding.

Sample Planning Calendar

Monday	Tuesday	Wednesday	Thursday	Friday
RI: Story structure and elements	RP: Story structure and elements	RI: Character traits	RP: Character traits	RI/RP: Character development
WI: Setting, character, and story sequences	WP: Setting, character, and story sequences	WI: Character traits V: Descriptive adjectives	WP: Character development V: Descriptive adjectives	WI/WP: Personal stories G: First vs. third person
RI: Conflict	RP: Conflict WI: Beginning, middle, and end G: Transitions	WP: Beginning, middle, and end WI: Openings and closings	RI: Summaries WI: Adding details V: Action verbs (show don't tell)	WP: Drafting
WP: Revising	RP: Comprehension check	WP: Editing G: Verb agreement TEST PREP	TEST PREP	TEST PREP

Legend

RI = Reading Instruction
RP = Reading Practice
WI = Writing Instruction
WP = Writing Practice
V   = Vocabulary
G   = Grammar

Strategy Overview: Setting the Scene

There are a number of decisions that a student must make before starting a story. Many students get stumped because they don't know what to write about. It is important for these students to use prewriting strategies to help them get lots of ideas on paper. Prewriting gives students interesting choices.

In this section, students play a game to practice stringing events together in a logical way using appropriate transitions. By giving careful consideration to the structure of a story, they can plan out the events and start to think about the causes and effects of those events.

The second lesson provides students with a way for inventing interesting characters by playing a game of matching traits with character types. This lets students practice exploring a character's possible traits and helps students see how traits support a character's type.

Use these lessons during the prewriting stage of the writing process to get students in a frame of mind for writing and to fill their word banks with rich and varied story choices.

Prewriting Mini-lesson: Story Structures

Materials

- Chart paper
- Timers (one for each pair of students)
- *Beginning-Middle-Ending Cards* (one set for each pair of students), pages 158–159
- *Story Tiles* activity sheet, page 160
- *Text Types and Purposes Chart*, page 26

Overview

Students will practice linking events together to create a story.

Planning

Review the terms *first, then, next,* and *last.* Have students practice describing their daily activities using these terms. When doing close reading, encourage students to discuss the story structure in terms of sequences of events. Use timelines for stories that include flashbacks or dream sequences.

Copy the *Beginning-Middle-Ending Cards* on two-sided paper, so that the fronts and backs align. Laminate the cards before cutting them out for sustainability.

Procedure

Modeling

1. Draw a three-column table on the board or a sheet of chart paper, and label the first column "beginning." Label the second column "middle" and the third column "ending." Introduce the terms *beginning, middle,* and *ending.* Ask students to define these terms and chart their answers.

2. Explain to students that the beginning of a story introduces the characters, the setting, and the problem or situation that the characters are facing. Add these ideas to the first column, and offer some sentence starters as examples of beginnings (e.g., *Once upon a time* or *One day...*).

3. Ask students to contribute one character, one setting, and a problem. Write their ideas on the board or use an overhead projector to model how to introduce these as the beginning of a story. For example, *One day, a prince was walking in the forest when he realized he was lost.* Ask students if this opening meets the criteria of a beginning.

4. Next, tell students that the middle of a story shows how the character makes some choices and has some experiences, all of which lead to the climax of the story. Guide students to add information about the middle of a story to the second column on the chart.

5. Ask students for two things that might happen to the prince before he finds his way home. For example, he might have to fight a troll, and he might meet a friend who has a magic compass. Take more suggestions and add them to the story that was started on the board. Model for students how to use transition words, such as "first," "then," and "next" as you write the story.

6. Ask students how the story might end. Explain that the ending is when the problem gets solved. For example, the prince might use the magic compass to find his way home, or he might capture the troll and have the troll lead the way.

7. Take suggestions from the students, and guide them to use the elements from the beginning and middle so that the story makes sense and is consistent. Write an ending for the story on the board. Use transitions words, such as "finally" or "at last."

Guided Practice

8. Tell students they will work with partners to build a story. Distribute the *Beginning-Middle-Ending Cards* to each pair of students, and have them place the three piles facedown.

9. One person starts by turning over the top card from each pile. The person then has one minute to combine the descriptions on each card into a short story and to think of an ending based on the conclusion words offered. If he or she can finish the story before the time runs out, he or she earns three points and the play passes to the next player.

10. If one of the cards simply doesn't work in the story, the player may elect to choose a different card but will forfeit a point.

Independent Practice

11. Have students use the *Story Tiles* activity sheets to draft their own story. They may use the cards to help them get started or invent an original story of their own.

12. Have students use the word bank to insert the appropriate transitions.

13. For an extra challenge, include blank cards and have students use their own ideas.

Reading Connection

As students are reading narratives, have them map the elements of the story on a blank *Story Tiles* activity sheet. Encourage students to highlight the transition words they encounter as they read. Use the activity sheets to help students write summaries of the stories they read.

Formative Assessment

If the student...	Consider practicing these prerequisite skills:
had trouble choosing transition words	provide additional word banks
had trouble choosing transition words	practice sequencing activities

Beginning-Middle-Ending Cards

Beginning	Beginning	Beginning
Beginning	Beginning	Beginning
Middle	Middle	Middle
Middle	Middle	Middle
Middle	Middle	Middle
Ending	Ending	Ending
Ending	Ending	Ending

 ©2016 Hillary Wolfe, MA from *Writing Strategies for the Common Core*. This page may be reproduced for classroom use only.

Beginning-Middle-Ending Cards

Who: Princess Where: Cloud city What: A lost crown	Who: A warrior Where: A distant planet What: A star is exploding	Who: A rhinoceros Where: The jungles of Africa What: Is smaller than the other rhinos
Who: A farmer Where: A farm What: The crops are dying	Who: A small kitten Where: A deserted alley What: Is being chased by a big dog	Who: A young child Where: Stuck inside on a rainy day What: A video game comes to life
An explosion…	A thunderstorm…	A dragon…
A kindly stranger…	A magic bottle…	A bird…
Electric currents…	Rocks…	A map…
Luckily,	Finally,	At last,
Sadly,	Phew! Hopefully,	Well, at least…

©2016 Hillary Wolfe, MA from *Writing Strategies for the Common Core*. This page may be reproduced for classroom use only.

Story Structures

Name: _____

Story Tiles

Directions: Fill in the chart below with who, where, and what information in the "Beginning" column, an event or two in the "Middle" column, and an idea for an ending in the "End" column. Use the "Transition Word Bank" to help you draft your ideas into a story.

Beginning	Middle	End
Who: Where: What:	First, Then,	Finally,

Transition Word Bank		

Once upon a time…
There once was…
In the beginning…
A long time ago…
It may surprise you
   to know that…
Did you ever
   wonder how…?
Welcome to…
	First,
	Before
	Then,
	Once
	Since
	When
	Because
	Next,
	Later,
	After that,
		Finally,
		In the end,
		After all of that,
		The last thing…
		So, the lesson
		   learned was…
		So always remember…
		And that's how…

Draft your story here. Use the back of this page as needed.

_____

_____

_____

 ©2016 Hillary Wolfe, MA from *Writing Strategies for the Common Core*. This page may be reproduced for classroom use only.

Prewriting Mini-lesson: Character Traits

Materials

- Chart paper
- Reading and Writing Portfolio
- *Types Cards* (one set for each group of 4 students), page 163
- *Traits Cards* (one set for each group of 4 students), page 164

Overview

Students will play a game to help them match character types with character traits.

Planning

Before the lesson begins, copy the *Types Cards* and *Traits Cards* onto card stock and laminate. Then cut as many as needed for each group to have one set.

Procedure

Modeling

1. Ask students to describe one of their favorite television characters. On a sheet of chart paper, draw a two-column chart. Label one column "Traits" and the other column "Types."

2. Sort the students' comments. Show them how physical traits are the characteristics we can see and personality types have to do with how the characters behave. Share some of their examples and have students discuss the traits that are on the chart.

3. Review the word *type*. Explain that we tend to make assumptions about the way characters behave based on some of their physical traits. For example, if we see a sweet-looking older woman, we tend to think of her as an affectionate grandmother *type*. While we shouldn't judge real people by how they look, storytellers take advantage of our reliance on types to help make a strong impression on the reader.

4. Tell students they are going to play a game where they get to match traits to a character type.

Guided Practice

5. Have students work in groups of four. Distribute one set of *Types Cards* and one set of *Traits Cards* to each group. For the game, one student will be the judge for each round. The judge deals three *Types Cards* to each player, then turns over one *Traits Card*.

6. Each player must choose a character type from his or her hand that would most likely exhibit the trait that was drawn. Players place the *Type Card* faceup and then must justify their choice for the judge.

7. After each player defends his or her choice, the judge picks the *Type* that most matches the *Trait*, and that player earns the *Trait Card*, winning the round. The role of the judge then passes to the next player on the right. Each player draws a new *Type Card* and play continues.

Independent Practice

8. Tell students they will work together to write a description of one of the character types from the game. Encourage students to use some of the traits from the game as they develop their character.

9. Have students work independently to create a short story about the character they described. Tell students to compare their stories and discuss which traits they chose and how the traits informed the story.

Reading Connection

As students read, have them use a note-taking guide that asks them to identify the traits that the characters display. Then, ask students to work with partners during shared reading to summarize the character types as they encounter them. As they read further, see if their opinions of the characters change or get stronger.

Formative Assessment

If the student...	Consider practicing these prerequisite skills:
had trouble identifying types	show pictures of familiar character types and use a word bank of adjectives to help students describe the characters

Types Cards

Movie Star	Sweet Grandmother	Cowboy	Techie	Race Car Driver
Hero	Football Player	Chef	Writer	Little Brother
Detective	Musician	Athlete	Surgeon	Cheerleader
Bride	Comic Book Villain	Brainiac	Artist	Pop Singer
Fairy Princess	Sailor	Sergeant	Spy	Pilot

©2016 Hillary Wolfe, MA from *Writing Strategies for the Common Core*. This page may be reproduced for classroom use only.

Traits Cards

Sweet	Whiny	Loud	Shy
Giggly	Snobby	Friendly	Giving
Embarrassed	Proud	Fearful	Brave
Smart	Patient	Bubbly	Excited
Nervous	Mysterious	Magical	Perfectionist

©2016 Hillary Wolfe, MA from *Writing Strategies for the Common Core*. This page may be reproduced for classroom use only.

Strategy Overview: A Compelling Situation

In addition to a logical sequence of events and interesting characters, a strong narrative centers around a compelling situation. Young students might need suggestions to get started with a story, but not every story needs to be fantastical. Simple ideas can be the start of a good story. Once students sketch out a sense of structure and develop interesting characters, they can start drafting a narrative. Start students with a first-person point of view since their own perspective is the most natural place to start telling a story. Then, challenge them to shift to a third-person narrator. The first lesson asks students to do a shared writing about a preselected topic from a perspective other than their own. Even though the topic is selected for the students, working with a partner allows the writing to be more spontaneous and encourages flexibility.

Next, students practice adding details by using a sensory spinner to insert realistic descriptions into a narrative. The goal is to help students understand the importance of descriptive details to add color and interest to a story.

This section shows how to draft a narrative by establishing a point of view and using rich descriptions to enhance a compelling situation. By combining all these elements, students will be on their way to writing successful and interesting narratives.

Drafting Mini-lesson: Shared Writing

Materials
- Chart paper
- Timer
- *Build a Story Activity Sheet,* page 168
- *Topic* cards (one set for each group of 4 students), page 169

Overview
Students will work collaboratively to create a narrative based on a predetermined topic.

Planning
Have students brainstorm some ideas independently before beginning their narratives. Once the story makes its way back to the original author, students can compare their plan with the story that was actually created. Prepare for this lesson by having available a few read-aloud stories that are written in the first-person point of view.

Procedure

Modeling

1. Choose a story written from the first-person point of view and read it aloud. Explain that the story is written from the point of view of the main character, which is called *first-person point of view.* Tell students that *first person* means the reader is experiencing the story from the perspective of the character, as if he or she were inside that character's thoughts.

2. Demonstrate how to tell a first-person story by narrating your trip to school this morning. Ask students what they notice about the word choices you make (e.g., using the word "I," only seeing things from one perspective). Chart their ideas and thoughts.

3. Remind students that a story must have a beginning, a middle, and an end. Ask students to describe the beginning, middle, and end of the story you just told or the story you read earlier. Chart some of the transition words they use.

4. Remind students that characters have certain traits that help us understand them. Ask students to describe the traits of the characters from the book you read earlier.

Guided Practice

5. Distribute one *Build a Story Activity Sheet* to each student.

6. Have students work in groups of four. Distribute one set of *Topic Cards* to each group.

7. Ask each student to choose one *Topic Card* and fill in the title on their *Build a Story Activity Sheet.* Have them write the opening line using the voice of the narrator written on the *Topic Card.*

8. Set a timer for three minutes. Tell students to start writing the beginning of the story that goes with the title until the timer goes off. Then have them pass their sheet to the person to their right.

9. Give everyone a chance to read what was written, and then set the timer again for another three minutes. Tell students to continue writing the story from the point where it left off until the timer goes off again.

10. Have students continue writing and passing until the story makes it back around to the original author.

Independent Practice

11. Ask students to read the story that was created. Give them time to ask clarifying questions of the members of their group about anything that doesn't make sense or isn't clear.

12. Set the timer one more time for seven minutes. Ask students to complete the story or to make any changes they want.

13. Have students volunteer to share their stories.

Reading Connection

As students are reading, have them identify the point of view of the narrator. Ask students to think about how the point of view impacts their understanding of the characters and the situation. How might a story be different if the reader saw a different perspective? Ask students to consider that there are often two sides to a story.

Formative Assessment

If the student...	Consider practicing these prerequisite skills:
had trouble starting a story	provide sentence frames with transition words
had trouble maintaining consistency	highlight key details about the setting, characters, or situation; trace the details through the story

Shared Writing

Name: _____

Build a Story Activity Sheet

Directions: Choose one *Topic Card*. Fill in the title on the line below, and fill in the name and description of the character on the card on the first line of the story.

Title: _____

Hello, my name is _____

and I am going to tell you about the day I _____

_____

_____

_____

_____

_____

_____

_____

_____

_____

_____

_____

_____

©2016 Hillary Wolfe, MA from *Writing Strategies for the Common Core*. This page may be reproduced for classroom use only.

Topic Cards

Title: The Day I Stayed with a Friend **Character**: Lucy the Mouse	**Title**: The Day I Found a Secret Room **Character**: Charles the Cat	**Title**: The Day I Stopped Being Afraid **Character**: Stanton the Pig	**Title**: The Day I Learned to Swim **Character**: Frankie the Fish
Title: The Day I Visited Grandma **Character**: Chester the Horse	**Title**: The Day of the Terrible Storm **Character**: Molly the Bumblebee	**Title**: The Day I Became Famous **Character**: Rocky the Boat	**Title**: The Day I Kept a Secret **Character**: Oliver the Owl
Title: The Day I Met My Best Friend **Character**: Cooper the Rocking Chair	**Title**: The Day I Learned to Play Piano **Character**: Vera the Centipede	**Title**: The Day of the Big Move **Character**: Stuart the Hermit Crab	**Title**: The Day I Overslept **Character**: Wally the Turtle
Title: The Day I Rode the Roller Coaster **Character**: Martin the Spider	**Title**: The Day I Got a Big Surprise **Character**: Molly the Balloon	**Title**: The Day I Met a Dolphin **Character**: Keisha the Seagull	**Title**: The Day I Traveled to the Moon **Character**: Pele the Banana
Title: The Day I… **Character**: (invent your own)	**Title**: The Day I… **Character**: (invent your own)	**Title**: The Day I… **Character**: (invent your own)	**Title**: The Day I… **Character**: (invent your own)

©2016 Hillary Wolfe, MA from *Writing Strategies for the Common Core*. This page may be reproduced for classroom use only.

Drafting Mini-lesson: Sensibility

Materials

- Scratch paper
- Chart paper
- Timers (one for each pair or group of 4 students)
- Reading and Writing Portfolio
- *Sensory Reference Cards,* pages 172–173
- *Sensibility Cards* (one set for each pair or group of 4 students), page 174
- *Show Me: A Riddle Poem* activity sheet, page 175

Overview

Students will practice including sensory details by playing a game that helps them think of descriptive terms. Then students will write a descriptive poem about a topic, including information from all five senses.

Planning

Laminate and cut the *Sensibility Cards* so that there are enough of each set for students to work in pairs or groups of four. Laminate the *Sensory Reference Cards,* and allow students to use dry-erase markers to add their own examples. Or create poster-sized versions of the *Sensory Reference Cards* to display around the room, with space for students to add ideas throughout the unit.

Procedure

Modeling

1. Post five sheets of chart paper. Label the sheets "Sight," "Sound," "Taste," "Touch," and "Smell."

2. Brainstorm aloud a few words for each sense. Ask students to work with a partner to brainstorm other examples of sensory words for each chart.

3. Have students write their ideas down on scratch paper, then come to the papers and post their best examples. Tell them not to post any repetitive words.

4. Review the words with students and confirm that they all agree about the appropriateness of the ideas. If a word doesn't seem to fit, ask students to justify the choices they made.

Guided Practice

5. Distribute copies of the *Sensory Reference Cards* to students. Tell students that when they play the game in a few minutes, they may refer to these cards for help. Ask students if they would like to add any ideas to the blank lines on the cards.

6. Have students work with partners or in groups of four. Distribute one set of *Sensibility Cards* to each pair or group, facedown. Explain the game: One player draws a card and holds it in front of him- or herself without looking at the word on the card. The other players have 30 seconds to describe the object listed on the card using sensory clues in the order outlined on the card until the first player guesses the object. The player gets one point for every "sense" that was needed to describe the object. Then, the next player draws a card, and play continues. The player with the least amount of points at the end of the game wins.

7. Ask students to add any sensory words that were particularly helpful to their reference cards or to the charts in the room.

Independent Practice

8. Distribute one copy of the *Show Me: A Riddle Poem* activity sheets to each student. Ask students to write a riddle poem about an object using all five senses to describe the object, without naming the object. Students may use objects from the *Sensibility Cards* or choose their own objects.

9. Have students trade papers with a partner and peer edit. Each poem should contain examples of descriptive words from all five senses.

10. Ask students to guess the object that their partners wrote about. Have students share their poems with the class.

Reading Connection

Have students highlight or underline examples of sensory words they find when they read. Have students keep a running list as they are reading about places, objects, or specific descriptions used in a text. Have students keep interesting examples of descriptive words and phrases in a pocket in their Reading and Writing Portfolios. Have students make flash cards with the word on one side and a sample sentence or drawing representing the sense on the other.

Formative Assessment

If the student...	Consider practicing these prerequisite skills:
had trouble identifying senses	colors, shapes, sizes, sounds, and basic taste words from a variety of print materials

Sensory Reference Cards

SIGHT	SOUND
bright	loud
colorful	soft
pretty	booming
shiny	screech
dark	squeaky
gloomy	whisper
see through	whirring
misty	beep
orange	ticking
glowing	tapping
tall	silent

 ©2016 Hillary Wolfe, MA from *Writing Strategies for the Common Core*. This page may be reproduced for classroom use only.

Sensory Reference Cards

TOUCH	TASTE	SMELL
moist	sour	sweet
sticky	spicy	fresh
wet	hot	flowery
slick	cold	smoky
bumpy	bitter	musty
smooth	smoky	fishy
slimy	lemony	pungent
soft	sweet	burnt
bouncy	tangy	spicy
rough	salty	citrusy
sharp	bland	earthy
pointy	burnt	fragrant

©2016 Hillary Wolfe, MA from *Writing Strategies for the Common Core*. This page may be reproduced for classroom use only.

Sensibility Cards

Pine Tree	Tissue	Pie
Taste	Sound	Sound
Sound	Taste	Touch
Touch	Smell	Sight
Smell	Sight	Smell
Sight	Touch	Taste
Mud	**Piano**	**Rain**
Sound	Taste	Smell
Taste	Smell	Touch
Smell	Touch	Sound
Sight	Sight	Taste
Touch	Sound	Sight
Jam	**Fire**	**Garbage Truck**
Sound	Sight	Taste
Touch	Sound	Touch
Smell	Smell	Sound
Sight	Touch	Sight
Taste	Taste	Smell
Cows	**Pizza**	**Food Court**
Touch	Smell	Sound
Smell	Taste	Touch
Sight	Sound	Sight
Taste	Sight	Smell
Sound	Touch	Taste

 ©2016 Hillary Wolfe, MA from *Writing Strategies for the Common Core*. This page may be reproduced for classroom use only.

Sensibility

Name: _____

Show Me: A Riddle Poem

Directions: Choose an object as the subject of your riddle. Then, write a poem that describes the object using all five senses, without naming the object. Share your poem with a partner and see if he or she can guess what you wrote about.

Object: _____

_____

_____

_____

_____

_____

_____

_____

_____

_____

_____

_____

_____

_____

Strategy Overview: Revising

A narrative unfolds through a series of events. These events may be presented in chronological order, relayed through flashbacks or dream sequences, or maybe even told from two perspectives. Keeping track of the sequence requires an effective use of temporal and transitional words that show order.

Young authors rely on formulas and structures when they are learning to craft their writing. While this is a sound practice, the danger is that students get stuck using repetitive phrases and predictable sentence structures because they don't have the confidence to try something else.

The revision lessons presented here challenge students to reread their own work and revise simplistic sentences by adding clauses that help sequence the events. By gaining experience and flexibility with interesting sentence structures, students are building a repertoire of interesting ways to tell a story.

One of the other challenges students face with writing is how to wrap up a story. Some students who don't know how to end a story will simply attribute the whole thing to a dream. Students need practice thinking of a closing event that will punctuate their narrative and give the reader a sense of closure. This revision lesson will also allow the student to tie the title to the closing event, which adds an element of suspense to the story by intriguing the reader.

Revising Mini-lesson: Sentence Complexity with Clauses

Materials

- Chart paper
- Reading and Writing Portfolios
- *Simple Sentence Cards* (one set for each group of 4 students), page 179
- *Clause Cards* (one set for each group of 4 students), page 180
- *Make It Complicated Score Sheet* (one for each group of 4 students), page 181

Overview

Students will play a game that helps them insert clauses into their writing in order to add sentence complexity and support a sequence of events.

Planning

Laminate and cut copies of the cards, or create your own simple sentences. Follow this activity by having students revise a piece of text they previously drafted. Ask them to find ways to change simple sentences into complex or compound sentences by adding clauses. Choose a piece of text from their Reading and Writing Portfolios.

Procedure

Modeling

1. On a sheet of chart paper, write a simple sentence, such as *The dog barked.* Identify for students the noun and verb in that sentence, and remind students that this is a simple sentence, meaning there is only one noun and one verb—one subject.

2. Tell students you want this sentence to answer the question, "When?" What would they need to add to this sentence? Guide students to add words such as, *when it heard the bell* or *after the package arrived.*

3. Write the words "adverb clause" on the chart paper. Tell students that adding an adverb clause to a sentence can provide more information, such as when an event took place or how the action happened. Draw columns for each question word or phrase: *when, where, why, how, how much,* and *under what condition.*

4. Define an adverb clause as a subject-and-verb combination that adds more information to a simple sentence. Have students practice adding adverb clauses to the question listed above in step 2. Chart their responses, and be sure to distinguish a clause from a phrase, which adds information but does not contain a subject and verb (e.g., *in the morning* or *after lunch*). A clause can help in storytelling because it can provide information that adds to a sequence of events (*when*) or provide more information about the action (*how*).

Guided Practice

5. Have students work in groups of four. Distribute one set of *Simple Sentence Cards* and *Clause Cards* to each group. Give each group a *Make It Complicated Score Sheet.* Have students write the names of all four players on the score sheet.

6. Explain the game. Each student is dealt three *Clause Cards.* One student will be the judge. The judge turns over one *Simple Sentence Card* and reads it aloud. The players must play a *Clause Card* and offer a clause that answers the question on their card in relation to the simple sentence. Each player presents his or her clause to the judge. The judge will choose the clause that makes the most sense. The player whose card is chosen wins the point for that round. Then, all players except the judge add their played cards to the bottom of the *Clause Card* pile and draw one new *Clause Card* (so they always have three in their hands). The role of the judge rotates to the next player, and play continues. The player with the most points wins the game.

Independent Practice

7. Have students choose a piece of text from their Reading and Writing Portfolios. Tell students to look for examples of simple sentences and circle any examples they can find.

8. Ask students to add adverb clauses to the examples that explain either *when, where, why, how, how much,* or *under what condition.* (Note: This can also be done with a piece of exemplar text from an online source or sample text that has been collected over time.)

9. Have students rewrite their drafts.

10. Tell students to trade papers with a peer and edit the work looking specifically for examples of adverb clauses. Students should underline the examples and identify the type of adverb clause used.

Reading Connection

As students read, have them continue to identify adverb clauses and distinguish what kind of information these clauses add to the text. Introduce noun clauses in the same way. Have them keep good examples of clauses in their Reading and Writing Portfolios.

Formative Assessment

If the student...	Consider practicing these prerequisite skills:
had trouble distinguishing phrases from clauses	nouns and verbs, subjects and predicates
had trouble distinguishing adverbs	provide word banks and sample starter phrases

Simple Sentence Cards

The dog barks.	The sun rises.	Breakfast is served.	Oranges grow on trees.
Kids ride bikes.	Doctors check for illness.	The dentist gives out toothbrushes.	Bears hibernate.
The moon glows.	Leaves fall.	Candles burn.	Rain clouds are forming.
Wear your ice skates.	The milk spilled.	A garden grows.	A bird flies.
The door slammed.	Cars speed.	A baby cries.	Brush her hair.

©2016 Hillary Wolfe, MA from *Writing Strategies for the Common Core*. This page may be reproduced for classroom use only.

Clause Cards

When?	When?	When?	When?
Where?	Where?	Where?	Where?
Why?	Why?	Why?	Why?
How?	How?	How?	How?
How much?	How much?	How much?	How much?
Under what condition?	Under what condition?	Under what condition?	Under what condition?

 ©2016 Hillary Wolfe, MA from *Writing Strategies for the Common Core*. This page may be reproduced for classroom use only.

Sentence Complexity with Clauses

Name: _____

Make It Complicated Score Sheet

Directions: Each student is dealt three *Clause Cards*. One student will be the judge. The judge turns over one *Simple Sentence Card* and reads it aloud. The players must play a *Clause Card* and offer a clause that answers the question on their card in relation to the simple sentence. Each player presents his or her clause to the judge. The judge will choose the clause that makes the most sense. The player whose card is chosen wins the point for that round. Then all players except the judge add their played cards to the bottom of the *Clause Card* pile and draw one new *Clause Card*. The role of the judge rotates to the next player, and play continues. The player with the most points wins the game.

Player 1	Player 2	Player 3	Player 4

©2016 Hillary Wolfe, MA from *Writing Strategies for the Common Core*. This page may be reproduced for classroom use only.

Revising Mini-lesson: Conclusions

Materials

- Chart paper (four sheets)
- Small whiteboard or large sticky notes (one for each of four equal student groups)
- Timer—optional
- *Choose an Ending* activity sheet, page 184

Overview

Students will work together in a fast-paced collaborative activity in which they compete to provide the best possible ending for a story. Students will learn four possible choices to end a narrative, allowing them to expand their options for writing conclusions.

Planning

Make sure the sheets of chart paper on which you will write ending techniques are large enough to be easily seen from around the room. This activity could be set up as a game between groups, with students using buzzers or bells or simply raising their hands quietly. Use timers to keep the activity quick and competitive.

Procedure

Modeling

1. Hang four sheets of chart paper in four different areas of the room, such as the four corners. Tell students that ending a narrative is sometimes tricky. Today they are going to learn four possible ways to wrap up a narrative or story.

2. On the first chart, write the words "Lesson Learned." Explain that some stories center around a character who learns an important lesson. Ask students to generate some examples, such as *Goldilocks and the Three Bears or The Three Little Pigs*. Ask students to explain the definition in their own words, and chart their responses as well as some examples from stories they have read.

3. On the second chart, write the words "Witty Reply." Tell students that some stories end with a funny comment, much like a punchline from a joke. For example, at the end of "Humpty Dumpty," when they can't mend him, one of the king's horsemen might console Humpty by saying, "Don't get so broken up about it." Ask students to explain the definition in their own words, and chart their responses as well as some examples from stories they have read.

4. On the third chart, write the word "Surprise." Tell students that a story might have a surprise ending, in which something totally unexpected happens. For example, Goldilocks could end up returning to the bears' house with some groceries and some wood glue to fix the chairs. Ask students to explain the definition in their own words, and chart their responses as well as some examples from stories they have read.

5. On the last chart, write the words "Funny Idiom" or adage. Explain that a familiar saying or an old adage (which is a proverb or short statement, like a familiar saying) can help wrap up a story. Students can use familiar idioms or make up silly ones. Fables are good examples of stories that end with an adage, such as the story of the tortoise and the hare: *Slow and steady wins the race*. Ask students to explain the definition in their own words, and chart their responses as well as some examples from stories they have read.

Guided Practice

6. Tell students they may take a moment and think about all the charts. Answer any questions they may still have about the four different ways they can end a narrative.

7. Have students select one chart to stand by. (If the groups are uneven, choose two or three students to participate as judges in addition to the teacher. Tell students that all the roles will be rotated, so every student can participate.) Tell students that you are going to read a series of familiar story plots, and it will be their job as a team to invent an ending that adheres to the definition on their chart. Model an example for each chart: For *Goldilocks and the Three Bears* at the "Lesson Learned" chart, students might say "Now she knows to not go into a house that doesn't belong to you!" For a *Witty Remark,* the story might end with "Goldilocks 'bearly' made it out of there alive!" For a *Surprise* ending, Goldilocks and the bears become best friends. And for the *Funny Idiom* ending, students could say "A bear in the house is worth two in the woods!"

8. Have students choose a representative who will speak for the group. Read aloud a familiar plot from *Choose an Ending,* and ask "Who can end this story?" Give students a chance to discuss in their groups, then write their "ending" on a small dry-erase board or chart paper.

9. Read the plot aloud again, and have each team take turns reading their ending. Student judges will score the endings on a scale of 1 to 4 (4 being best). After a couple of rounds, rotate teams so that they all have a chance to be at different charts or serve as judges. At the end of the game, the team with the most points wins.

Independent Practice

10. Have students revisit a narrative draft from their Reading and Writing Portfolios. Ask students to rewrite their ending using one of the four techniques offered in this mini-lesson.

11. Have students trade papers with a peer, showing both the original paper and the revised version. Peers should be honest about which ending is better and why.

12. Have students complete this activity by creating a title and/or cover picture for their writing. The title and/or picture should relate to the conclusion.

Reading Connection

As students read, have them identify different types of endings used by authors. Students should practice using similar conclusion techniques in their own writing and discuss the conclusions of their paragraphs.

Formative Assessment

If the student...	Consider practicing these prerequisite skills:
did not understand one or more of the terms	sentence starters, such as "Now I know..." or "It just goes to show..."

Choose an Ending

Directions: Explain four different ways students may end a story. Then, choose one of the familiar plots from the list below, and have students create an ending. Give points for the most inventive or appropriate ending. Have students rotate so that they each have an opportunity to explore all four types of endings.

Lesson Learned	Witty Reply
Surprise	Funny Idiom

With the help of magic, a poor girl goes to a ball and falls in love with a handsome prince. Her evil stepmother tries to stop them from getting together.

A turtle and a rabbit have a race. The turtle goes slow but never stops. The rabbit, on the other hand, is very fast but easily distracted.

A puppet maker carves a boy out of wood. A magic spell brings the boy to life, but he makes bad choices and ends up in some big trouble. He is almost doomed to stay a wooden character forever, which would break his father's heart.

A chicken needs help baking bread. She asks all her friends to help gather the wheat, make the grain, mix the dough, and bake the bread, but no one will help her. When the bread is done, all her friends are hungry and ask her to share.

Three pigs build houses. One is made of sticks, one of straw, and one is made of bricks. Soon, a hungry wolf comes along and wants to get his paws on these pigs.

Two children get lost in the woods. They use breadcrumbs to leave a trail to get home, but the birds eat the crumbs. They come upon a house made of candy, but it belongs to a witch, who captures them both.

©2016 Hillary Wolfe, MA from *Writing Strategies for the Common Core*. This page may be reproduced for classroom use only.

Culminating Project Ideas

Language Arts

Write a narrative about someone who has been a best friend to you, the most difficult thing you've ever learned to do, or your favorite vacation day ever. Include pictures or diagrams in your narrative.

Texts:

A Dog Called Prince by Jay Dale (fiction), published by Capstone

Courageous Children by Jane Bingham (nonfiction), published by Capstone

Social Studies

Become an imaginary pen pal to a famous historical figure. Write what this figure would tell you about his or her life, including major events and important people.

Texts:

Boys Who Rocked the World: Heroes from King Tut to Bruce Lee by Michelle Roehm McCann and David Hahn (fiction), published by Turtleback

Heroes of the American Revolution by Mary Hertz Scarbrough (nonfiction), published by Capstone

Leading the Way by Mary Lindeen (nonfiction), published by Capstone

Mathematics

Write a detective story about the adventures of a number as it encounters Addition, Subtraction, Multiplication, and Division characters. Consider how these mathematical concepts translate into narrative actions, such as quests or conflicts.

Texts:

Basher Basics: Math: A Book You Can Count On by Simon Basher (nonfiction), published by Kingfisher

Fractions in Disguise: A Math Adventure (Charlesbridge Math Adventures) by Edward Einhorn (fiction), published by Charlesbridge

Science

Write a diary from the perspective of a plant (starting from a seed) or a drop of rain. Include important science content that demonstrates conceptual understandings as well as an understanding of story structure.

Texts:

Drew Drop and the Water Cycle by Cathy Sherman (fiction), published by CreateSpace Independent Publishing Platform

Ghosts and Atoms by Jodi Wheeler-Toppen (nonfiction), published by Capstone

The Little Drop of Water Who Learned to Give Himself Away by Jerry D. Kaifetz, Ph.D. (fiction), published by CreateSpace Independent Publishing Platform

©2016 Hillary Wolfe, MA from *Writing Strategies for the Common Core*. This page may be reproduced for classroom use only.

Additional Resources

Essay Frames

Opening Paragraph
Grabber: Use a zoom-in, close-up description or a sound effect.
(Ex.: Each drop of rain hit the window like a grenade. Boom! Boom! Boom!)

_____

_____

Transition to topic: Give context to this detail, transitioning to the story.
(Ex.: It was my first soccer game of the season, and even the weather was out to get me.)

_____

_____

Transition to thesis and main idea: Look back at the topic sentences of your body paragraphs. Use the main ideas you chose as evidence to complete the introduction paragraph.
(Ex.: It was the hardest thing I've ever done, but with a supportive coach and a belief in myself, my first soccer game turned out to be something I'll never forget.)

_____

_____

_____

_____

_____

_____

_____

_____

 ©2016 Hillary Wolfe, MA from _Writing Strategies for the Common Core_. This page may be reproduced for classroom use only.

Body Paragraph Frame

I. **Topic Sentence:** Restate the main idea from your opening paragraph. (Ex.: When a coach believes in you, you start to believe in yourself, and before you know it, you're scoring goals.)

_____

_____

1. **Describe or define** what you mean. Describe in order the events that happened.

   _____

   _____

   _____

2. **Explain** what happened in your own words. Think of answering questions such as *how*, *when*, and *where*.

   _____

   _____

   _____

3. Use a line of **dialogue** that was said during the incident.

   _____

   _____

   _____

4. **Define** the context of this quote, and explain how it demonstrates an important part of the story.

   _____

   _____

   _____

©2016 Hillary Wolfe, MA from *Writing Strategies for the Common Core*. This page may be reproduced for classroom use only.

II. **Closing sentence:** Use a conclusion word or an adverb to end this paragraph. (Ex.: Clearly, winning a game is a team effort.)

_____

_____

_____

HOMEWORK: USE THIS WORKSHEET TO WRITE YOUR BODY PARAGRAPHS—
DUE TOMORROW!

 ©2016 Hillary Wolfe, MA from *Writing Strategies for the Common Core*. This page may be reproduced for classroom use only.

Closing Paragraph

Respond to grabber: Continue the imagery from the close-up you used in the opening paragraph. (Ex.: Tap. Tap. Tap. The drops of rain on the car windshield sounded like clapping. The game was over, and now the falling rain sounded like applause.)

_____

_____

Restate the topic. (Ex.: Anytime you do something hard for the first time, you take a chance that it will go very badly.)

_____

_____

Restate the thesis and main ideas. (Ex.: It's amazing how much a good coach can help you believe in yourself.)

_____

_____

Clincher: What is your last word about this topic? (Ex.: Now I know, keep fighting, even when things get hard, because you can achieve your goals.)

_____

_____

Title: Use words from your clincher. (Ex.: "Goals")

_____

_____

©2016 Hillary Wolfe, MA from _Writing Strategies for the Common Core_. This page may be reproduced for classroom use only.

Rubrics: Point-based

Directions: Assign points for any or all of the following elements; or, focus on one or two elements or paragraphs at a time, and have students revise their work to earn additional points.

Format — _____ points

    Three paragraphs (introduction,
       one body paragraph, conclusion)   _____

    Typed or handwritten in ink   _____

    Proper indentation   _____

    Spelling/punctuation   _____

Writing Process/Materials — _____ points

    Transition worksheet   _____

    Body paragraph worksheet   _____

    Body paragraph rough draft   _____

    Opening/Closing paragraph worksheet   _____

    Opening/Closing paragraph rough draft   _____

    Peer edit/Self-edit   _____

Opening Paragraph — _____ points

    Close-up or sound effect   _____

    Topic   _____

    Thesis   _____

    Main ideas   _____

Body Paragraph — _____ points

    Topic sentence starts with an adverb   _____

    Topic sentence addresses main idea   _____

    Describe the main idea using sequences   _____

    Explain how the events support the main idea   _____

    Use a quote to offer more explanation   _____

    Closing sentence with adverb   _____

Closing Paragraph — _____ points

    Complete the close-up or sound effect   _____

    Restate topic in different words   _____

    Restate thesis and main idea   _____

    Clincher   _____

    Title (matches clincher)   _____

©2016 Hillary Wolfe, MA from *Writing Strategies for the Common Core*. This page may be reproduced for classroom use only.

Analytic Rubric

	Above Average (4)	Sufficient (3)	Developing (2)	Needs Improvement (1)
Develops real or imagined experiences or events using effective technique, descriptive details, and clear event sequences				
Establishes a situation and introduces a narrator and/or characters; organizes an event sequence that unfolds naturally				
Uses narrative techniques, such as dialogue, description, and pacing, to develop experiences and events or show the responses of characters to situations				
Uses a variety of transitional words, phrases, and clauses to manage the sequence of events				
Uses concrete words and phrases and sensory details to convey experiences and events precisely				
Provides a conclusion that follows from the narrated experiences or events				
Produces clear and coherent writing in which the development, organization, and style are appropriate to task, purpose, and audience.				
Develops and strengthens writing as needed by planning, revising, editing, rewriting, or trying a new approach, focusing on how well purpose and audience have been addressed				

©2016 Hillary Wolfe, MA from *Writing Strategies for the Common Core*. This page may be reproduced for classroom use only.

	Above Average (4)	Sufficient (3)	Developing (2)	Needs Improvement (1)
Uses technology, including the Internet, to produce and publish writing and link to and cite sources				
Draws evidence from literary or informational texts to support analysis, reflection, and research				

 ©2016 Hillary Wolfe, MA from *Writing Strategies for the Common Core*. This page may be reproduced for classroom use only.

Holistic Rubric

4	The student writes narratives that orient the reader by establishing a situation and introducing the narrator and characters. The writer organizes an event sequence that unfolds naturally; the writer uses dialogue and description to develop experiences and events and shows the responses of the characters to different situations. A variety of transitional words and phrases manage the sequence of events. Concrete words and phrases and sensory details convey experiences and events. A clear conclusion follows from the narrated experiences or events. The writing demonstrates exemplary command of the conventions of standard written English.
3	The narrative adequately establishes a situation, narrator, and characters, but the reader is not fully oriented to the narrative. The event sequence is logical, with minimal dialogue and some details and descriptions that develop experiences and events. Transition words are used. There is a conclusion to the events. Minimal errors do not detract from overall meaning and understanding.
2	The narrative does not clearly establish a situation, a narrator, and characters. The reader is confused by the event sequence. Superficial descriptions and details, including minimal dialogue and character development, leave holes in the narrative. The organization is present but is not thoughtful or cohesive. There are several noticeable misspellings and mechanical errors.
1	The narrative is unclear; a sequence of events, an established narrator, and character development is lacking. There is little relationship between the events, and the sequence is unclear. There is no evidence of effective transition words. Misspellings and mechanical errors are frequent and detract from the ability to comprehend the work.

(Adapted from *Assessment: Types of Rubrics, DePaul University*)

©2016 Hillary Wolfe, MA from *Writing Strategies for the Common Core*. This page may be reproduced for classroom use only.

Chapter **6**

Test Prep

Overview: Dissecting a Prompt

On-demand writing can be intimidating for young students, especially those who lack confidence as writers. Being given a limited amount of time to write about an unfamiliar subject can be very stressful. Students may freeze up, panic, or resort to a rudimentary, formulaic writing style. Worst of all, students may simply resign themselves to a poor grade.

Purpose

The testing process can be just as frustrating for teachers. Despite working tirelessly with students on all the steps of the writing process, the on-demand test requires a frenetic synthesis of weeks and weeks' worth of information, without the benefits of peer editing, revision, or even prewriting. The writing students have done in class had been explicitly described; the sources they used had been scrupulously analyzed; the rubric was clear and outlined exactly what they were to include. On-demand writing gives students none of these supports. One of the first stumbling blocks is simply understanding the prompt.

Fortunately, students can be given strategies that will help them understand what the prompt is asking and guide them as to how to prepare for writing. They can learn how to use the prompt as their road map to quick organization so that when they start to write, they already have a working rough draft in their heads. If they need to cite from a text that is provided, they can do so confidently because they will know what kind of evidence they are looking for.

The three lessons in this section are meant to be taught individually but ultimately practiced all together as a prewriting exercise, so students gain a flexibility and comfort with the process. The lessons show students how to:

- Determine the task and the purpose of the writing assignment,
- Manipulate the language of the prompt to create their thesis statements, and
- Use clues from the prompt (either explicit or implied) to sketch out supporting ideas.

Test Prep Strategy: Determine the Task

Focus: Structure and Verbs

Prompts are often structured in a confusing way. Read the (fictional) example below:

Read the following passage about pets:

> *Dogs and cats make great pets. They are loving and loyal. Dogs come in all sizes. Besides being great playmates, dogs can be helpful caregivers too. For example, some dogs are service dogs for people with illnesses. Some dogs are working dogs, helping on farms or pulling sleds in snow. Cats are fun pets too. They are cuddly and playful, and they can help scare away mice and rodents. Pets are good additions to a family.*
>
> *Which do you think is the better pet to have? Write a paragraph about the best pet. Use evidence from the text above. Be sure your writing has a clear beginning, middle, and end.*

Notice how the text that is to be cited offers a few bits of factual information but not enough to necessarily make a determination. There is little context offered. A cat might be the best pet for someone who lives in an apartment, while a large dog would fare better living where there is access to the outdoors. Without experience, students are likely to ignore the text and base their writing on their personal opinions. They will need to be taught to return to the text to find and cite examples that back up their opinions. They will need practice to determine how to structure their writing and to recognize that the word "better" is an indication that this is to be an argument paragraph. It is important to give students these opportunities so they know what they are being asked to do before they begin writing.

As a caveat, if you plan on providing test prep practice, it is advisable to turn to the released questions from previous years' tests rather than trying to write your own, unless you can successfully mirror the style and format of the actual test. It is important to provide a prompt for practice that is similar to what students will actually experience. Sample tests for most states can be found online, usually with scoring guides and annotations.

Test Prep Strategy: Create a Thesis

Focus: The Prompt Is the Key

Once students understand what they are being asked, they must quickly create a thesis statement and decide how they will support their claims. This can be difficult under pressure, especially if the prompt centers on a topic about which the students have little experience or knowledge. Again, it is important that students have a plan of action so they don't panic in these situations.

Students need to be shown how to use the information provided in the prompt to create a viable thesis. They don't have to know much about the topic. The test is not assessing their conviction; it is assessing their ability to write a cohesive, well-organized piece with evidence cited from the text as well as other examples.

Introduce strategies that allow students to objectively pull their thesis from the prompt and show them how to quickly get started rather than using up valuable minutes deciding how they feel about the topic.

Focus: Outline Your Ideas

Remember the fictional example from the previous page? The student may not like either cats or dogs, or they may be allergic to both. Regardless, the text gives them some help as to how to support their thesis: Dogs make good pets because of the services they provide; cats also can be helpful. Each of these reasons could easily become main supporting ideas, giving the student a viable outline for an essay.

Prerequisite Skills

As you complete each of the units in this resource, consider a few days of test prep around that specific text type, so students experience an immediate application of the skills they will need to proficiently write on demand. After completing the unit on explanatory writing, review with students the types of explanatory writing (process, cause and effect, etc.), types of transition words, and what constitutes a strong supporting detail. Show them how to use their portfolios to help them select a writing structure that is appropriate for the text type. Refer students to their own work as you introduce the three test prep lessons.

Genre-specific Vocabulary

Teach students the signal words that will indicate the type of essay they will be expected to write. For example, if they are to write an explanatory essay, the prompt will use terms, such as *explain, show, outline, describe how, tell about a process, sequence,* or *describe the steps.* The prompt for an argument might ask students very explicitly to *argue for* or *convince,* but it may also use terms like *write a letter in which you persuade...,* or *choose the best....* A narrative essay may ask students to *discuss, reveal, share,* or *examine* and will usually involve personal feelings. Unless students have been taught to recognize the signals, they will not be confident about completing the task appropriately.

Strategy Overview: Dissecting the Prompt

Test prep often implies a complete practice test that students can complete without pressure. These experiences are helpful for students as they expose them to the time constraints and the testing environment as a dry run, but logistically, it can be a time-consuming process for the teacher. How many days can the teacher devote to test prep in this manner? Realistically, even if a teacher provides three or four opportunities for students to write a practice essay, they are still getting only minimal exposure to the types of questions they may be asked in an actual testing situation.

By breaking down the test prep into smaller pieces, teachers can help students construct a simple series of steps that can be applied to multiple testing situations. If students have a playbook of strategies, they won't feel as panicky when faced with a real testing situation. Moreover, smaller instructional components mean the test prep can be woven into regular instruction more frequently.

In soccer, practice consists of regularly repeating simple drills, combined with authentic application opportunities. These test prep exercises represent the drills, and once students master the processes, the drills can be repeated often, as bell work, at stations, for homework, or as extension activities. In this way, students have multiple exposures to the types of questions they will be asked on high-stakes tests and will hopefully experience less trepidation in actual testing situations.

The text prep exercises have been separated into individual lessons for explanatory/informational, argument, and narrative text types. The test prep could follow the unit to which it aligns. It is also possible to combine information about all three types of essays into one lesson. All of the lessons follow very similar process steps so that students gain familiarity with the procedure of breaking down a prompt to discern the task and to start planning an appropriate response.

Test Prep Mini-lesson: Determine the Task (Explanatory/Informational)

Materials

- Sample explanatory writing prompts
- Chart paper
- Document camera
- *Dissecting a Prompt Note-taking Guide* (three per student), page 200
- *My Turn Graphic Organizer* (several per student), page 201

Overview

Students will brainstorm synonyms for task-oriented words they are likely to find in test prompts and determine how those words inform the content and structure of an essay. Students will practice distinguishing the verbs in sample prompts that identify and define the tasks. Note: As students become more proficient at this strategy, combine the test prep passages to offer more varied exposure to different types of essay prompts.

Planning

Find sample prompts from your state test's released questions, or use the Appendix items from the Common Core State Standards (corestandards.org) to display and use for student practice. Have prompts that represent different text types. Note: Instead of using note-taking guides and graphic organizers, students can use individual whiteboards to create a graphic organizer or keep the information under a "Test Prep" tab in their Reading and Writing Portfolios. Or slip the graphic organizer into a sheet protector and have students use wipe-off markers for the guided and independent practice portions of the lesson.

Procedure

Modeling

1. Access students' prior knowledge by posting a large sheet of chart paper. Write the word "Explain" at the top. Draw a three-column chart on the sheet. Distribute copies of the *Dissecting a Prompt Note-taking Guide* to each student. Think aloud about words that are synonymous with *explain* (for example, *tell, describe,* or *show*). Write the synonymous words in the first column on the chart.

2. Label the first column "Verb." Have students write "Explain" on their first note-taking guide, on the line labeled "Text Type." Ask students to work with partners to brainstorm additional words and add them to their note-taking guides. Write some of their suggestions on the chart.

3. Label the second column "Means...." Remind students that an explanatory essay is one in which the author explains *how, why,* or *which.* Write these words in the second column. Then tell students these words help determine a specific text structure: *how* means the essay will present a process, a sequence, or a series of steps; *why* means the essay will explain a cause and effect or a problem and solution; and *which* means the essay will require a comparison. Write these descriptions on the chart paper under the "Means..." column, and have students add them to their note-taking guides.

4. Label the third column "Plan to Use…." Remind students that explanatory essays have very specific structures, which means they require specific elements. Write "Transition Words" in the third column, and ask students to supply the types of transition words that they remember using for processes, sequences, causes and effects, comparisons, and descriptive or spatial text structures. Add these words to the chart, and have students add them to their note-taking guides.

Guided Practice

5. Distribute copies of the *My Turn Graphic Organizer.*

6. Display a sample writing prompt using a document camera or on an interactive whiteboard. Highlight or circle the verbs in the prompt. Have students fill in the verbs, in the same order that they appear, in the first box on their graphic organizers.

7. Model how to translate the verb into a task by referring to the *Dissecting a Prompt Note-taking Guide.* For example, if the verb is *Describe,* the task is to write an explanatory essay. Ask students to highlight the verb or verbs that identify the actual task the prompt is stating, and to articulate the task in the next box on the graphic organizer.

8. Display another prompt, and ask students to work with partners to identify the verb and then translate it into a task using their note-taking guides as reference.

Independent Practice

9. Have students complete all boxes on the graphic organizer using additional prompts.

10. Ask students to write an explanation of the types of tasks these prompts were describing and to articulate their thinking about how they were able to determine the task. Note: Use sentence frames as necessary to ensure that students are using the appropriate academic vocabulary.

11. Have students turn in their explanations as a ticket out the door.

Formative Assessment

If the student...	Consider practicing these prerequisite skills:
struggled with text structures	transition words
struggled with the verbs	synonyms of active verbs

Dissecting a Prompt Note-taking Guide

Name: _____

Directions: Fill in the chart below.

_____
(Text Type)

Verb	Means...	Plan to use...

 ©2016 Hillary Wolfe, MA from *Writing Strategies for the Common Core*. This page may be reproduced for classroom use only.

My Turn Graphic Organizer

Name: _____

Directions: Read the sample prompt. Highlight or circle the verbs. Then fill in the chart below.

Verbs:
Task:
Because of the verb(s) _____ this essay is a(n) _____ essay. Therefore, I will plan to use _____ in my essay.
Verbs:
Task:
Because of the verb(s) _____ this essay is a(n) _____ essay. Therefore, I will plan to use _____ in my essay.

Test Prep Mini-lesson: Determine the Task (Argument)

Materials

- Sample argument writing prompts
- Chart paper
- Document camera
- *Dissecting a Prompt Note-taking Guide* (three per student), page 200
- *My Turn Graphic Organizer* (several per student), page 201

Overview

Students will brainstorm synonyms for task-oriented words they are likely to find in test prompts and determine how those words inform the content and structure of an argument. Students will practice distinguishing the verbs in sample prompts that identify and define the tasks.

Planning

Find sample prompts from your state test's released questions, or use the Appendix items from the Common Core State Standards (corestandards.org) to display and use for student practice. Have prompts that represent different text types. Note: Instead of using note-taking guides and graphic organizers, students can use individual whiteboards to create a graphic organizer or keep the information under a "Test Prep" tab in their Reading and Writing Portfolios. Or slip the graphic organizer into a sheet protector and have students use wipe-off markers for the guided and independent practice portions of the lesson.

Procedure

Modeling

1. Access students' prior knowledge by posting a large sheet of chart paper. Write "Argument" on the sheet. Draw a three-column chart on the sheet. Distribute copies of the *Dissecting a Prompt Note-taking Guide* to each student.

2. Think aloud about words that are synonymous with *persuade* (for example, *convince, tell, argue for...*). Write the synonyms in the first column on the chart. Label the first column "Verb." Have students write "Argument" on their note-taking guide, on the line labeled "Text Type." Ask students to work with partners to brainstorm additional words and add them to their note-taking guides. Write some of their suggestions on the chart.

3. Label the second column on the poster "Means...." Tell students that an argument essay will require the writer to present examples, both personal and based in evidence from text, that will convince an audience of a particular point of view or position. Write this description on the chart paper under the "Means..." column, and have students label the column and add this description to their note-taking guides.

4. Label the third column "Plan to Use...." Remind students that argument essays also have very specific characteristics. Write "Audience," "Tone," and "Types of Support" in the third column. Ask students to supply types of audiences (peers, authority), tones (formal, casual, angry), and different types of support (facts, expert opinions, data, personal examples) that they remember using for arguments. Place these words in the chart, and have students add them to their note-taking guides.

5. Distribute copies of the *My Turn Graphic Organizer.*

6. Display a sample writing prompt using a document camera or an interactive whiteboard. Highlight or circle the verbs in the prompt. Have students fill in the verbs, in the same order that they appear, in the first box on their graphic organizers.

7. Model how to translate the verb into a task by referring to the *Dissecting the Prompt Note-taking Guide.* Ask students to highlight the verb or verbs in the prompt that identify the task to complete and to articulate the task in the next box on the graphic organizer.

8. Display another prompt, and ask students to work with partners to identify the verb and then translate it into a task using their note-taking guides as reference.

Independent Practice

9. Have students complete all boxes on the graphic organizer using additional prompts.

10. Ask students to write an explanation of the types of tasks these prompts were describing and to articulate their thinking about how they were able to determine the task. Note: Use sentence frames as necessary to ensure that students are using the appropriate academic vocabulary.

11. Have students turn in their explanations as a ticket out the door.

Formative Assessment

If the student...	Consider practicing these prerequisite skills:
struggled with persuasive techniques	facts, opinions, and personal examples
struggled with tone	audience, point of view, and purpose
struggled with word choice	strong action verbs and cohesive language

Test Prep Mini-lesson: Determine the Task (Narrative)

Materials

- Sample narrative writing prompts
- Chart paper
- Document camera
- *Dissecting a Prompt Note-taking Guide* (three per student), page 200
- *My Turn Graphic Organizer* (several per student), page 201

Overview

Students will brainstorm synonyms for task-oriented words they are likely to find in test prompts and determine how those words inform the content and structure of an essay. Students will practice distinguishing the verbs in sample prompts that identify and define the tasks.

Planning

Find sample prompts from your state test's released questions, or use the Appendix items from the Common Core State Standards (corestandards.org) to display and use for student practice. Have prompts that represent different text types. Note: Instead of using note-taking guides and graphic organizers, students can use individual whiteboards to create a graphic organizer or keep the information under a "Test Prep" tab in their Reading and Writing Portfolios. Or slip the graphic organizer into a sheet protector and have students use wipe-off markers for the guided and independent practice portions of the lesson.

Procedure

Modeling

1. Access students' prior knowledge by posting a large sheet of chart paper. Draw a three-column chart. Distribute copies of the *Dissecting a Prompt Note-taking Guide* to each student.

2. Think aloud about words that are synonymous with *narrate* (for example, *describe, discuss, tell about a time...,* or *show*). Write the synonymous words in the first column on the chart. Have students write "Narrate" on their first note-taking guide, on the line labeled "Text Type." Ask students to work with partners to brainstorm additional words and add them to their note-taking guides. Write some of their suggestions on the chart.

3. Label the second column on the poster "Means...." Remind students that a narrative essay will require the writer to reveal a lesson learned, a challenge that was overcome, or an influential person or event that altered the writer's perspective. Write this description on the chart paper under the "Means..." column, and have students label the column and add this description to their note-taking guides.

4. Label the third column "Plan to Use...." Remind students that narrative essays may have unusual structures, but they still have some common characteristics. Write "Beginning," "Middle," and "End" in the third column. Ask students to describe how a narrative (biographical or a story) might begin (by introducing the characters, setting, and conflict), what might happen in the middle (the rising action, the events that lead to the climax), and what might happen in the end (the resolution). Add these descriptions

to the chart, and have students add them to their note-taking guides.

5. Write "Characters" and "Details" in the third column. Ask students to remember that characters are described physically and also through dialogue and actions that give clues about their personalities. Remind students about the kinds of sensory details that help the reader visualize the events in a story.

Guided Practice

6. Distribute copies of the *My Turn Graphic Organizer*.

7. Display a sample writing prompt using a document camera or on an interactive whiteboard. Highlight or circle the verbs in the prompt. Have students fill in the verbs, in the same order that they appear, in the first box on their graphic organizers.

8. Model how to translate the verb into a task by referring to the *Dissecting the Prompt Note-taking Guide*. Ask students to highlight the verb or verbs that identify the actual task in the prompt and to articulate the task in the next box on the graphic organizer.

9. Display another prompt, and ask students to work with partners to identify the verb and then translate it into a task using their note-taking guides as reference.

Independent Practice

10. Have students complete all boxes on the graphic organizer using additional prompts.

11. Ask students to write an explanation of the types of tasks these prompts were describing and to articulate their thinking about how they were able to determine the task. Note: Use sentence frames as necessary to ensure that students are using the appropriate academic vocabulary.

12. Have students turn in their explanations as a ticket out the door.

Formative Assessment

If the student...	Consider practicing these prerequisite skills:
struggled with sequencing	transition words, timelines, descriptive text structures
struggled with character descriptions	dialogue, physical traits, sensory descriptions, point of view

Test Prep Mini-lesson: Create a Thesis (Explanatory/Informational)

Materials
- Sample explanatory writing prompts
- Highlighters
- *Building a Thesis Graphic Organizer,* pages 208–209

Overview
Students will use information presented in the prompt as the foundation for their thesis statements.

Planning
Find sample prompts from your state test's released questions, or use the Appendix items from the Common Core State Standards (corestandards.org) to display and use for student practice. Have prompts that represent different text types. Note: Instead of using note-taking guides and graphic organizers, students can use individual whiteboards to create a graphic organizer or keep the information under a "Test Prep" tab in their Reading and Writing Portfolios. Or slip the graphic organizer into a sheet protector and have students use wipe-off markers for the guided and independent practice portions of the lesson.

Procedure
Modeling

1. Connect to students' prior knowledge by reminding them of the work they have done in using the verbs in a prompt to identify the task they are being asked to complete. (Have students refer to the independent practice sheets from the previous lesson.) Remind students that a thesis is different from a topic, in that it represents the position the author will take about the topic.

2. Distribute copies of the *Building a Thesis Graphic Organizer* to students. Display the sample prompt that appears on the students' worksheets. Use a highlighter to call out the verbs in the prompt: *read, explain, compare, contribute.* Ask students which verbs identify the task (*read, explain, compare*).

3. Underline the nouns surrounding the task verbs (*two pieces of text, structure, main idea*). Ask students to underline these nouns on their own sheets and to write the phrases in the "Task" box on their graphic organizers. Have students identify the type of essay this prompt is suggesting (explanatory, compare). Model and think aloud: *"Compare* means finding the similarities and differences."

4. Ask students to identify the topic of the essay ("the theme of two texts"). Have them write the topic on their graphic organizers.

5. Model how to craft the thesis by returning to the prompt. Think aloud as you write on the displayed copy of the graphic organizer: "If I have to *compare,* one piece of text uses a structure that supports the theme in a different way from the other piece of text. That is how I will start my thesis. I will write (as an example): *The sequenced structure of the first text makes me know it is explaining a process, but the descriptive structure of the second text tells me it is describing an event.*" Have students write a thesis statement in the "Thesis" box on their graphic organizers.

6. Tell students that a thesis statement should also include an introduction to the supporting ideas that will be presented in the essay. These supporting main ideas will make up the topics for the body paragraphs. Typically, an explanatory essay will have two or three supporting paragraphs, which means the student must determine what the main ideas of these paragraphs will be and express them along with the thesis.

7. Tell students the main ideas will most likely also come from the prompt. "In this case, the body paragraph should explain one way the two texts are similar and one way the texts are different." Have students share out and write their responses in the "Main Idea" boxes on their graphic organizers.

Guided Practice

8. Display a new prompt, and have students use the second graphic organizer to fill in the verbs, the task, and the topic. Have them work with a partner to craft a thesis.

9. Tell students to use two different colors to highlight phrases from the prompt that might indicate two supporting main ideas. Have them share and discuss with a partner.

10. Ask students to write their main ideas on their graphic organizers.

Independent Practice

11. Repeat this process as necessary using new prompts and blank graphic organizers.

Formative Assessment

If the student...	Consider practicing these prerequisite skills:
struggled with identifying the task	active verbs, explanatory text structures
struggled with finding main ideas	creating word webs and identifying synonyms

Building a Thesis Graphic Organizer

Name: _____

Directions: Read the sample prompt below. Highlight the verbs and determine the task. Write the task in the chart below. Identify the topic. Then craft your thesis, and add the topics for the supporting paragraphs.

Read two pieces of text. Explain the structure of each. Then compare the two texts and explain how the structures contribute to an understanding of each text's main idea.

Verbs:	Task:
Topic:	
Thesis:	
Main Idea 1:	**Main Idea 2:**

©2016 Hillary Wolfe, MA from *Writing Strategies for the Common Core*. This page may be reproduced for classroom use only.

Building a Thesis Graphic Organizer (cont'd.)

Name: _____

Directions: Read the sample prompt. Highlight the verbs and determine the task. Write the task in the chart below. Identify the topic. Then craft your thesis, and add the topics for the supporting paragraphs.

Verbs:	Task:
Topic:	
Thesis:	
Main Idea 1:	**Main Idea 2:**

©2016 Hillary Wolfe, MA from *Writing Strategies for the Common Core*. This page may be reproduced for classroom use only.

Test Prep Mini-lesson: Stake Your Claim (Argument)

Materials

- Sample argument writing prompts
- Highlighters
- *Building a Claim Graphic Organizer,* pages 212–213

Overview

Students will use information presented in the prompt as the foundation for their claims.

Planning

Find sample prompts from your state test's released questions, or use the Appendix items from the Common Core State Standards (corestandards.org) to display and use for student practice. Have prompts that represent different text types. Note: Instead of using note-taking guides and graphic organizers, students can use individual whiteboards to create a graphic organizer or keep the information under a "Test Prep" tab in their Reading and Writing Portfolios. Or slip the graphic organizer into a sheet protector and have students use wipe-off markers for the guided and independent practice portions of the lesson.

Procedure

Modeling

1. Connect to students' prior knowledge by reminding them of the work they have done in previous lessons using the verbs in a prompt to identify the task they are being asked to complete. (Have students refer to the independent practice sheets from the previous lessons.) Remind students that a claim is different from a topic, in that it represents the position or point of view about a topic.

2. Distribute copies of the *Building a Claim Graphic Organizer* to students. Display the sample prompt that appears on the students' worksheets. Use a highlighter to call out the verbs in the prompt: *change, improve, write, use, support.* Ask students which verbs identify the task (*write, support*).

3. Underline the important phrases surrounding the task verbs (*write a letter, explaining what you would change, support your ideas*). Ask students to underline these phrases on their own sheets and to write the phrases in the "Task" box on their graphic organizers. Have students identify the type of essay this prompt is suggesting (argument). Model and think aloud: "*Explaining what you would change* means this essay will need to convince the reader to change or improve something in the school."

4. Tell students that all the information they need to state their claims is in the prompt.

5. Ask students to identify the topic of the essay ("think about what you would change or improve in your school"). Have them write the topic on their graphic organizers. Model how to craft the thesis by returning to the prompt. Think aloud as you write on the displayed copy of the graphic organizer: "If I have to *choose one thing to change,* my claim must state some problem I see at school. I will choose to add more trees to the playground. I will write: *If I could make one change to the school, I would plant more trees on the playground.*" (Note: As a revision exercise, ask students to restate this claim

in a more creative way; e.g., *One thing that would really improve our school would be extra shade on the playground.*) Have students brainstorm some other things they would change, and write a claim in the "Claim" box on their graphic organizers.

6. Tell students that a claim should also include the reasons why the author is stating this opinion. These reasons will become the topics for the body paragraphs. Typically, an argument essay will have two or three supporting paragraphs, which means the student must determine what the main ideas of these paragraphs will be and express them along with the claim.

7. Tell students the prompt will likely offer ideas about the kind of evidence to use. In this case, the body paragraphs should explain at least two reasons why the student chose a particular thing to change. Ask students what is one reason they would make the change they suggest and how would they go about it? Have students share out and write their responses in the "Main Idea 1" box on their graphic organizers.

8. Ask students what is one more reason they would make this change? Have students share out and write their responses in the "Main Idea 2" box on their graphic organizers.

Guided Practice

9. Display a new prompt, and have students use the second graphic organizer to fill in the verbs, the task, and the topic. Have them work with a partner to craft a claim.

10. Tell students to use two different colors to highlight phrases that might indicate two different types of evidence they could find to support their claims, including personal examples and facts. Have them share and discuss with a partner.

11. Ask students to write their main ideas on their graphic organizers.

Independent Practice

12. Repeat this process as necessary using new prompts and blank graphic organizers.

Formative Assessment

If the student...	Consider practicing these prerequisite skills:
struggled with identifying the task	review synonyms and the definition of *persuade*
struggled with choosing evidence	review purpose and audience and show how those impact tone and word choice

Building a Claim Graphic Organizer

Name: _____

Directions: Read the sample prompt below. Highlight the verbs and determine the task. Write the task in the chart below. Identify the topic. Then state your claim, and add the main ideas for the evidence in the supporting paragraphs.

What is one thing you would like to change or improve about your school? Write a letter to your principal explaining what you would change, why you would change it, and how you would change it. Use reasons and evidence to support your ideas.

Verbs:	Task:
Topic:	
Claim:	
Main Idea 1:	**Main Idea 2:**

©2016 Hillary Wolfe, MA from *Writing Strategies for the Common Core*. This page may be reproduced for classroom use only.

Building a Claim Graphic Organizer (cont'd.)

Name: _____

Directions: Read the sample prompt. Highlight the verbs and determine the task. Write the task in the chart below. Identify the topic. Then craft your claim, and add the topics for the supporting paragraphs.

Verbs:	Task:
Topic:	
Claim:	
Main Idea 1:	**Main Idea 2:**

©2016 Hillary Wolfe, MA from *Writing Strategies for the Common Core*. This page may be reproduced for classroom use only.

Test Prep Mini-lesson: Plot and Character (Narrative)

Materials

- Sample narrative writing prompts
- Highlighters
- *Explaining Plot and Character Traits Graphic Organizer,* pages 217–218

Overview

Students will use information presented in the prompt to explain plot and character traits.

Planning

Find sample prompts from your state test's released questions, or use the Appendix items from the Common Core State Standards (corestandards.org) to display and use for student practice. Have prompts that represent different text types. Note: Instead of using note-taking guides and graphic organizers, students can use individual whiteboards to create a graphic organizer or keep the information under a "Test Prep" tab in their Reading and Writing Portfolios. Or slip the graphic organizer into a sheet protector, and have students use wipe-off markers for the guided and independent practice portions of the lesson.

Procedure

Modeling

1. Connect to students' prior knowledge by reminding them of the work they have done in using the verbs in a prompt to identify the task they are being asked to complete. (Have students refer to the independent practice sheets from the previous lesson.) Remind students that explaining plot and character traits will help shape how they address the topic.

2. Distribute copies of the *Explaining Plot and Character Traits Graphic Organizer* to students. Display the sample prompt that appears on the students' worksheets. Use a highlighter to call out the verbs in the prompt: *describe, helped, were helped.* Ask which verb identifies the task (*describe*).

3. Underline the other important words or phrases (*helping each other, circumstances, characteristics*). Ask students to underline these words and phrases on their own sheets and to write them in the "Task" box on their graphic organizers. Have students identify the type of essay this prompt is suggesting (narrative). Model and think aloud: "*Describe a time* means this will be a personal narrative essay."

4. Ask students to identify the topic of the essay ("friends helping each other"). Think aloud to model how to decide what situation to write about, e.g., working on a project for school, fixing something that was broken, training for a baseball game. Give students a few minutes to brainstorm some ideas. Have them write the topic they decide upon on their graphic organizers.

5. Model how to establish a situation by returning to the prompt. Think aloud as you write on the displayed copy of the graphic organizer: "If I have to *describe a time,* my point of view must be first person. It will be about me. What is a situation that happened to me that stands out?" (Note: If the prompt asked students about another person, the point of view might be third person.)

6. Model how to introduce the characters and organize the sequence of events. Think aloud: "*Characters* means I have to provide information about who else was involved in the situation. I have to describe who they were and give some information about their personality traits that helps paint a clear picture for the reader. I will write, *When I was 8* (tells when and who), *I fell off my bike and had to miss three weeks of baseball practice* (tells what happened). *Thanks to my strict coach and my competitive best friend* (tells a little about their personality types), *I was able to work hard and start the season opener.* (Note: As a revision exercise, ask students to restate this thesis in a more creative way; e.g., *It's funny how one spill on a bike can really hurt your batting average and how a good friend can get you back in the game.*) Have students write about a situation in the box on their graphic organizers that establishes situation and characters.

7. Tell students that a narrative should also include an introduction to the supporting ideas that will be presented in the essay. These supporting main ideas will make up the topics for the body paragraph. A narrative essay could have any number of body paragraphs, but the structure should include a clear beginning, middle, and end.

Guided Practice

8. Tell students the prompt will often give clues about what to include in the supporting paragraphs. On the display, use a different color to highlight the following: *benefit from working together and helping each other.* The beginning of the narrative must include information about the situation, what the problem was, and who helped you through it, or how you helped a friend through a tough situation. For instance, in the baseball example, a student might write: *I loved riding my bike, and my friend and I spent the whole summer riding together. He helped me by teaching me tricks on my bike and shortcuts around the neighborhood. When I broke my ankle, my friend taught me how to practice my swing, even if I had to do it sitting down!* Have students brainstorm and share out some of their responses, and have them add this information to the "Beginning" box on their graphic organizers.

9. Ask students, what other types of information they should include in their narratives. (Students should indicate that they should identify some of the challenges that they encountered.) Have students share out and write their responses in the "Middle" box on their graphic organizers.

10. Use a different color to highlight the following on the display: *What are some of the characteristics of a helpful person?* Ask students, based on this question, what is another element that should be included in the middle? (Students should indicate that they should identify the ways people were helpful.) Have students brainstorm and share out, then write their responses in the "Middle" box on their graphic organizers.

11. Finally, tell students the ending of the essay should represent the climax and resolution of the essay. In this case, the ending should explain how the problem was finally overcome, what the student learned through this experience, and what the benefits were. Have students brainstorm and share out. Ask them to write their responses in the "End" box on their graphic organizers.

Independent Practice

12. Display a new prompt, and have students use the second graphic organizer on their sheets to fill in the verbs, the task, and the topic. Have them work with a partner to determine a situation and the characters.

13. Tell students to use different colors to highlight phrases that might indicate what to include in the beginning, middle, and end. Have them share and discuss with a partner.

14. Ask students to write their main ideas on their graphic organizers.

15. Repeat this process as necessary using new prompts and blank graphic organizers.

Formative Assessment

If the student...	Consider practicing these prerequisite skills:
struggled with conflict	character traits
struggled with beginning, middle, and end	story structure and story elements
struggled with point of view	first- and third-person perspectives

Explaining Plot and Character Traits Graphic Organizer

Name: _____

Directions: Read the sample prompt below. Highlight the verbs and determine the task. Write the task in the chart below. Identify the topic. Then determine the situation and character traits, and add the information you will include in the beginning, middle, and end of the narrative.

> *People can benefit from working together and helping each other. Describe a time you either helped someone, or were helped by a friend. What were the circumstances? What are some of the characteristics of a helpful person?*

Verbs:	Task:
Topic:	

Situation and Character Traits:

Beginning:	Middle:	End:

©2016 Hillary Wolfe, MA from *Writing Strategies for the Common Core*. This page may be reproduced for classroom use only.

Explaining Plot and Character Traits Graphic Organizer (cont'd.)

Name: _____

Directions: Read the sample prompt. Highlight the verbs and determine the task. Write the task in the chart below. Identify the topic. Then determine your point of view and the context, and add the information you will include in the beginning, middle, and end of the narrative.

Verbs:	Task:
Topic:	
Situation and Character Traits:	

Beginning:	Middle:	End:

 ©2016 Hillary Wolfe, MA from *Writing Strategies for the Common Core*. This page may be reproduced for classroom use only.

Quick-Reference Writing Guide

	Expository			Persuasive	Narrative	Response to Literature
	Process	Compare/Contrast	Cause & Effect			
PURPOSE	To explain...how	To explain...which (choose)	To explain...why	To convince	To reveal	To react
AUDIENCE	Academic	Academic	Academic	Peer/Academic	Peer/Academic	Academic
SIGNAL WORDS IN THE PROMPT	Explain how..., Put in order..., Show how..., Describe the steps...	Compare..., Decide which..., Choose..., Relate...	List the causes..., Tell why..., Show why..., Give the reasons..., What will happen when...	Convince..., Argue..., Persuade..., Promote..., Defend..., Prove...	Tell about a time when..., Remember a situation when..., Have you ever wanted/felt/wished..., How do you feel about...	Respond to..., React..., Give your reaction/feelings about..., What would you do if...
TRANSITIONS/ LANGUAGE/	First, after, later, soon, until, and then, next, eventually, finally	Also, both, likewise, similarly, as well as, although, even though, instead of, on the other hand, however, despite	As a result, so, because, so that, for this reason, therefore, if...then, thus, since, whenever	It follows, furthermore, moreover, again, consequently, therefore, of course, necessarily, clearly, without a doubt	Later, when, before, then, in a while, another thing, after, as if, I learned, now I know, next time	Another example, just as, in the same way as, reinforced by, underscoring, in addition to
	Specific, clear, descriptive	Analogous, parallel structures	Parallel, logical progressions, clear connections	Active verbs, emotional, impassioned, imperatives, cohesive and thematic adjectives	Emotional, revealing, sensitive, touching, heartrending, honest, sincere	Specific, descriptive, illustrative, tied to text
TRY THIS GRABBER FOR OPENING	Simile or three questions	Simile or three questions	Statistic or three questions	Three questions	"In the moment" or "sound effect" personal anecdote with a connection to the thesis	Quote from the piece with an analysis that connects to the thesis
WAYS TO SUPPORT THE MAIN IDEA	1. Describe or explain 2. Make a comparison 3. Show cause and effect 4. Make a prediction	1. Describe or explain 2. Show cause and effect 3. Make a prediction 4. Show the relationship	1. Describe or explain 2. Compare 3. Predict 4. Deduce 5. Give personal example or quote a source	1. Describe or explain 2. Compare 3. Show cause and effect 4. Predict 5. Use one or two propaganda techniques	1. Describe or explain 2. Compare or connect 3. Show cause and effect 4. Predict 5. Give personal examples 6. Evaluate/give judgment	1. Quote-Analysis 2. Describe/explain 3. Compare/connect 4. Cause/effect OR literary technique
MOST IMPORTANT THING TO REMEMBER	Be simple and specific: use clear, logical order	Find the relationship; distinguish fact from opinion	Clearly relate one event to the next	Be assertive and sure	Be vulnerable and reflective	Use evidence from the text and always explain why you chose it and what it means

References

ACT (2005). Crisis at the core: Preparing all students for college and work. Retrieved from http://www.act.org/research/policymakers/pdf/crisis_report.pdf Feb. 25, 2012.

Allington, R. & Gabriel, R. (2012, March). Every child, every day. *Educational Leadership, 15*(1), 10–15.

Alvermann, D. E. (2002). Effective literacy instruction for adolescents. *Journal of Literacy Research, 34*. 189–208. doi: 10.1207/s15548430jlr3402_4.

Aud, S., Hussar, W., Kena, G., Bianco, K., Frohlich, L., Kemp, J. & Tahan, K. (2011). *The Condition of Education 2011* (NCES 2011-033). U.S. Department of Education, National Center for Education Statistics. Washington, DC: U.S. Government Printing Office.

Bandura, Albert. (1997). *Self-efficacy: The exercise of control.* New York: Freeman.

Berman, I. (2009). Supporting adolescent literacy achievement. Issue Brief. NGA Center for Best Practices. February 25, 2009. Retrieved from http://carnegie.org/fileadmin/Media/Publications/PDF/0902ADOLESCENTLITERACY.PDF May 20, 2012.

Biancarosa, G. (2012, March). Adolescent literacy: More than remediation. *Educational Leadership, 15*(1), 22–27.

Bitter, C., O'Day, J., Gubbins, P. & Socias, M. (2009): What works to improve student literacy achievement? An examination of instructional practices in a balanced literacy approach. *Journal of Education for Students Placed at Risk (JESPAR), 14*(1). 17–44.

California Department of Education (2012). Curriculum Frameworks, English Language Arts, para. 1. Retrieved from http://www.cde.ca.gov/ci/rl/cf/ May 20, 2012.

California State Board of Education (2010, Aug.). State Board Meeting. Agenda Items August 2, 2010. Retrieved from www.cde.ca.gov/be/ag/ag/yr10/agenda201008.asp April 18, 2012.

City-Data.com (2009) Retrieved from http://www.city-data.com/school/california-city-middle-ca.html April 15, 2012.

Cohan, George M. "Over There." Leo Feist, Inc., 1917.

Cohle, D. & Towle, W. (2001). *Connecting reading and writing in the intermediate grades: A workshop approach.* Newark, DE: International Reading Association.

Common Core State Standards Implementation Plan for California (2012, March). Retrieved from California Department of Education, Common Core State Standards Resources, http://www.cde.ca.gov/ci/cc/index.asp May 20, 2012.

Common Core State Standards Initiative. (2011). Retrieved from http://www.corestandards.org/ Feb. 26, 2012.

Conley, D. T., Drummond, K. V., de Gonzalez, A., Rooseboom, J. & Stout, O. (2011). Reading the goal: The applicability and importance of the Common Core State Standards to college and career readiness. Eugene, OR: Educational Policy Improvement Center. Retrieved from http://www.epiconline.org/publications/documents/ReachingtheGoal-FullReport.pdf May 20, 2012.

Cooper, J. D., Kiger, N. D., Robinson, M. D., Slansky, J. A. & Au, K. H. (2011). *Literacy: Helping students construct meaning.* Independence, KY: Cengage Learning.

Cunningham, P. M. & Allington, R. L. (1999). *Classrooms that work: They can all read and write.* New York: Longman.

Deshler, D. D. & Hock, M. F. (2006). *Shaping Literacy Achievement.* New York: Guilford Press.

Duke, N. K., Caughlan, S., Juzwik, M. M. & Martin, N. M. (2012, March). Teaching genre with purpose. *Educational Leadership, 15*(1), 34–39.

Eckert, L. S. (2008). Bridging the pedagogical gap: Intersections between literary and reading theories in secondary and postsecondary literacy instruction. *Journal of Adolescent & Adult Literacy, 52*(2). 110–118.

Framework for 21st Century Learning (2009). Partnership for 21st Century Skills. Retrieved from http://www.p21.org/storage/documents/P21_Framework.pdf Feb. 25, 2012.

Franzak, J. (2006, Summer). Zoom: A review of the literature on marginalized adolescent readers, literacy theory, and policy implications. *Review of Educational Research 76*(2). 209–248.

Graham, S. & Hebert, M. (2010). Writing to read: Evidence for how writing can improve reading. *A Report from Carnegie Corporation of New York.* New York: Alliance for Excellent Education.

Graham, S. & Perin, D. (2007). Writing next: Effective strategies to improve writing of adolescents in middle and high schools. *A Report from Carnegie Corporation of New York.* New York: Alliance for Excellent Education.

Guccione, L. M. (2011, May). Integrating literacy and inquiry for English learners. *The Reading Teacher, 64*(8). 567–577.

IRA/NCTE (1996). *Standards for the English Language Arts.* Newark, DE: International Reading Association; Urbana, IL: National Council of Teachers of English.

Lyon, G. E. (1993). "Where I'm From." *Stories I Ain't Told Nobody Yet.* New York: Theater Communications Group.

Mermelstein, L. (2006). Excerpted from *Reading/writing connections in the K–2 classroom: Find the clarity and then blur the lines* (pp. 56–68). Columbus, OH: Allyn & Bacon. Retrieved from http://www.education.com/reference/article/components-balanced-literacy/ February 28, 2012.

Miller, M. & Veatch, N. (2010, Nov.). Teaching literacy in context: Choosing and using instructional strategies. *The Reading Teacher, 64*(3). 154–165.

National Reading Panel (2000, April). Teaching children to read: An evidence-based assessment of the scientific research literature on reading and its implications for reading instruction. *Report of the National Reading Panel.* U.S. Department of Health and Human Services. Retrieved from http://www.nichd.nih.gov/publications/pubs/nrp/pages/smallbook.aspx May 1, 2015.

Partnership for 21st Century Skills (2011). www.p21.org. Accessed May 20, 2012.

Pearlman, B. (2009, Sept.–Oct.). Making 21st century schools. *Educational Technology.* 14–19. Retrieved from www.bobpearlman.org.

Porter-Magee, K. (2012). Getting Common Core implementation right: The $16 billion question. Common Core Watch. Thomas B. Fordham Institute. Retrieved from http://www.edexcellence.net/commentary/education-gadfly-daily/common-core-watch/2012/getting-common-core-implementation-right-the-16-billion-question.html May 20, 2012.

Saulnier, B. (2008). From "Sage on the Stage" to "Guide on the Side" revisited: (Un)Covering the content in the learner-centered information systems course. *Information Systems Education Journal, 7*(60), 1–10.

Schunk, D. H. (2003). Self-efficacy for reading and writing: Influence of modeling, goal setting, and self-evaluation. *Reading & Writing Quarterly 19,* 2: 159–172

Schunk D. H. & Parajas, F. (2005). Chapter 6 Competence perceptions and academic functioning. In *Handbook of Competence and Motivation,* 85–104. New York: The Guilford Press.

Schunk, D. H. & B. J. Zimmerman. (2007). Influencing children's self-efficacy and self-regulation of reading and writing through modeling. *Reading & Writing Quarterly 23,* 1: 7-25.

Swafford, J. & Durrington, V. A. (2010). Middle school students' perceptions: What teachers can do to support reading self-efficacy. *Building literacy communities. Association of literacy educators and researchers yearbook,* Vol. 32. Louisville, KY: Bellarmine University, 221–235.

Sweeny, S. M. (2010, Oct.). Writing for the instant messaging and text messaging generation: Using new literacies to support writing instruction. *Journal of Adolescent & Adult Literacy, 54*(2), 121–130. doi:10.1598/JAAL.54.2.4.

The Albert Shanker Institute (2011, Spring). A call for common content. *American Educator, 35*(1), 41–45.

U.S. Department of Education (1999a). U.S. Department of Education's 1999 Performance Report and 2001 Annual Plan. Vol. 1. Retrieved from http://www2.ed.gov/pubs/AnnualPlan2001/index.html May 20, 2012.

U.S. Department of Education (1999b) U.S. Department of Education's 1999 Performance Report and 2001 Annual Plan. Vol. 1. Retrieved from http://www2.ed.gov/pubs/AnnualPlan2001/index.html May 20, 2012.

Vacca, J. L, Vacca, R.T., Gove, M. K., Burkey, L.C., Lenhart, L. A. & McKeon, C. A. (2003). *Reading and learning to read.* Akron, OH; Allyn & Bacon.

Wiggins, G., & McTighe, J. (2008, May). Put understanding first. *Educational Leadership, 65*(8), 36–41.

Wiggins, G. & McTighe, J. (2011). *The Understanding by Design guide to creating high-quality units.* Alexandria, VA: ASCD. Accessed on Understanding by Design® Framework, http://www.ascd.org/ASCD/pdf/siteASCD/publications/UbD_WhitePaper0312.pdf April 15, 2012.

Wilhelm, J., Baker, T. & Dube, J. (2001). *Strategic reading: Guiding students to lifelong literacy*. Portsmouth, NH: Heinemann. Excerpted at http://www.myread.org Feb. 26, 2012.

Wisconsin Department of Public Instruction. "What is the NCLB?" and ten other things parents should know about the No Child Left Behind Act. http://esea.dpi.wi.gov/files/esea/pdf/parents.pdf. Accessed Feb. 25, 2012.

Maupin House *by*
capstone
professional

At Maupin House by Capstone Professional, we continue to look for professional development resources that support grades K–8 classroom teachers in areas, such as these:

Literacy	Language Arts
Content-Area Literacy	Research-Based Practices
Assessment	Inquiry
Technology	Differentiation
Standards-Based Instruction	School Safety
Classroom Management	School Community

If you have an idea for a professional development resource, visit our Become an Author website at:

http://maupinhouse.com/index.php/become-an-author

There are two ways to submit questions and proposals.

1. You may send them electronically to:
    http://maupinhouse.com/index.php/become-an-author

2. You may send them via postal mail. Please be sure to include a self-addressed stamped envelope for us to return materials.

Acquisitions Editor
Capstone Professional
1 N. LaSalle Street, Suite 1800
Chicago, IL 60602